A formal patio pond

Other titles in this series:

An **INTERPET** *Guide to*

Garden
Ponds

A fully planted semi-formal pond

An informal garden pond

An **INTERPET**  *Guide to*

Garden Ponds

An easy-to-follow practical guide to constructing,
stocking and maintaining a pond in your garden

David Papworth

INTERPET

An **INTERPET** Book

©1999 Interpet Publishing
Vincent Lane, Dorking,
Surrey RH4 3YX,
United Kingdom.

ISBN 1-902389-54-9

A garden pond in spring

Credits

Editor: Geoff Rogers
Design: Tony Dominy
Colour reproductions:
Tempus Litho
Filmset: SX Composing DTP
Printed in China

Author

David Papworth is a freelance writer and illustrator on horticultural subjects. For a period of 12 years he was Gardening Editor of Ideal Home magazine and was Editor of The Water Gardener magazine from its launch until 1995. David has written several books, including *Patios and Water Gardening* and *Patios and Windowbox Gardening*, and guides to bulbs and conifers. He regularly contributes articles and illustrations to gardening and DIY books and magazines.

Consultant
Fascinated by fishkeepeing from early childhood, Dr. Neville Carrington devised an internationally known liquid food for young fishes while studying for a pharmacy degree. After obtaining his Doctorate in Pharmaceutical Engineering Science and a period in industry, Dr. Carrington pursued his life-long interest in developing equipment and chemical products for the aquarium world.

Contents

Introduction

If there is one thing that gives more satisfaction than a garden full of flowers, shrubs and trees, it is a garden that has all these plus some water, whether it is a pond, a lake or a stream. A simple pond should provide clear water with bright reflections, the movement of fishes and a chance to grow the exotic-looking aquatic plants, some of which are heavily scented. Using simple methods of pond construction, you can make a delightful place of interest in your garden, a centre point of conversation that fascinates visitors and draws all eyes. Apart from the pond itself, there is the animal life that it attracts, from insects to amphibians.

The sound of water in summer is very soothing: on a hot, lazy day when everything is still apart from the hum of insects, the splash of water from a fountain or waterfall recreates the atmosphere of more tropical scenes. The glitter of water gives movement to an otherwise static garden, and attracts birds to drink and bathe.

With a pond we can learn more about nature and the section of life that lives in water or is closely allied to it, with its balance of one

animal feeding on another and yet supplying food to a different species to form a cycle of life and death, with each member an important link in the chain. We can study fishes, insects, amphibians and other forms of animal life that are attracted to the pond; how they grow, change and mature; what they eat and how they benefit the other pond occupants; and why some live close to the surface and are easily seen, while others lurk in the depths.

Plants are also very interesting in their growth patterns from seed or dormant root; some thrive and dominate their area, whereas others are slower and seem to struggle for life. A plant may produce a vast quantity of foliage and few flowers, yet another will have a tremendous show of colourful blooms with the minimum of leaf growth. It is interesting to watch flowers progress from buds to full blooms, being pollinated and producing ripe seeds to reproduce their species. Other plants increase their numbers by running roots under ground or under water, and producing sprouts of foliage some distance from the parent plant.

Design and location

The placing of the pond is important: to position it in the wrong area can be a disaster, giving rise to many problems and plenty of regrets. If you place it near deciduous trees, a shower of leaves every autumn will fall into the water and pollute it. In the shade, the flowers will not open as well as they would in the sunshine. If you plant the wrong kind of plants around and in the pond, you won't be able to see the water for foliage; and if you stock the pond with the wrong fishes there could be an aquatic battleground until the strongest clears the pond of the weaker members.

It is very rewarding to have considered the pond's shape and size and the livestock and achieved a successful balance. A fine display will give pleasure to your visitors, and you will feel that your efforts have been worth while. If the water area is unusual in shape and style, you have the satisfaction of knowing that the pond is unique, and of watching it mature and develop over the years.

If you choose the right method of containing the water, there should be a long period of trouble-free enjoyment without having to keep checking that the liner is not becoming degraded and brittle, that retaining walls are perhaps not quite strong enough and should those cracks really be there? You must also decide whether to have a below-ground or an above-ground pond, what size and type of pump to buy, and whether to have a little light at night or to go the whole hog and put in floodlights (with underwater ones as well) so that you can enjoy evening viewing and entertaining.

The design of the pond should take into consideration the space around the water and how it should be seen and used: will there be

plenty of space for people to walk around and view the fishes and plants, or will there be any hazards that could cause someone to trip; is there a place for sitting near the pool; and can your pool be viewed from the house when the weather is not warm or dry? By asking these questions you can make the design functional and practical, and once constructed the pond will give years of interest, pleasure and instruction for the whole family.

Planting

To list suitable plants for the pond owner to choose from in the limited space available in this book is bound to result in some omissions, but this is a selection that will give some variety in type, season, size and colour, and for shallow and deep water as well as boggy conditions. The plant list has been divided into sections for easy selection (with the water lilies listed separately because they form such a large group), and the sections are put into separate lists according to size, and then into colours. The choice is based on the plants that are readily available and suitable for the pool, and that will grow in the temperate areas of the world.

Some common plants are very invasive, and where necessary they have been left out because they could spoil the pond where space is restricted. Other plants that are very vigorous have been left in, if it is easy to grow them in a container to stop them spreading and taking over the whole pond. Obviously it would need a vast complex of ponds to contain all the listed plants, but the list will give the pond owner a wide choice of different types; start with half a dozen and increase the varieties as the pond matures.

Fishes

The fishes have been selected in the main to give the new owner a taste of what is available: they include the decorative varieties with bright colours and the not so decorative fishes that are important because they clean the pool of unwanted rubbish. Some will become tame enough to eat out of your hand and show themselves whenever you appear. But make sure that the fishes and other livestock are suitable before introducing them into the pond, so that no one species will dominate and attack the other inhabitants. The obvious example is the Pike – also known by its apt name, Freshwater Shark – which will clear a pond of other fishes very quickly.

Keep the fish food near the water so that it can be given easily when the fishes are active. If you supplement the food with earthworms, do wash them under a tap to remove impurities before mincing or chopping them and dropping them into the water. Keep the pond understocked to begin with, as the fishes will grow and

need more food and oxygen. It is very easy to overstock, and it will look fine while there is plenty to eat and the weather is cool, but when the temperature soars the water will become deoxygenated, causing the fishes distress. This can be seen when the fishes start to swim with their heads close to the surface. It is best to lift some out and put them in a separate tank or pond until the water cools and the oxygen levels have risen.

The other forms of livestock can provide hours of interest, with the smaller members such as the flies and beetles giving so much energy to their search for food, and the snail is such a contrast as it steadily moves around. Although the pond will give hours of fascination to the older child in the life-cycles of fishes and insects, take care to inform the very young child of the dangers of water; it is the visitor who is at most risk, as ignorance of the hazards can result in accidents. The owner who is aware of this fact usually makes sure that young visitors are supervised until they realise the danger.

Water

To most people water is a simple liquid with a chemical basis of two hydrogen atoms combining with one of oxygen; but in nature it can vary considerably, as natural water contains other chemicals and organisms that can change its properties. Those waters with a high lime content are referred to as hard water, whereas low lime waters are referred to as soft. This is due to rain falling on soils that have a high or low lime content and picking up minerals as they filter through the layers of soil. Near volcanic vents, the minerals saturate the water to produce waters rich in sulphur or magnesium.

Tap water may also have other additions; chlorine and fluoride are probably the two best known, but even in soft-water areas some authorities add lime to make the water less acid. Rain water can present problems if you live to the windward of certain factories that emit fumes with a high sulphur content; these fumes can combine with water vapour in the air to form sulphuric acid and cause what is known as 'acid rain', which has left lakes in Scandinavia left clear blue but totally devoid of life.

The quality of pond water

If you want to keep fishes, water is a vital factor, and it must be able to support life without causing suffering. To use tap water, it is necessary to allow the chlorine to disperse, which it will do if left for a week or so before any plants or fishes are introduced into the pond. There are various forms of testing kits available that have been developed for pond use, and these can be used to register the chemical level and the balance of the water. A simple test is to watch the health of the plants and fishes; if they thrive, the water is reasonably balanced; but if the fishes become a poor colour, show no sign of growth and move sluggishly, then the water is suspect.

If water is left static, it becomes stagnant. The mineral salts in the water act together with sunlight and encourage the primitive plant life called algae and the proliferation of free-swimming green organisms,

Above: *The sea evaporates to form clouds of water vapour that fall on cooler high ground as rain.*

Above: by testing the water, the acidity or alkalinity can be determined and balanced as needed.

which make the water look green; eventually they die and start to putrify, using up oxygen and producing toxic gases. On the other hand, if the water is partially shaded to keep out some of the sunlight (usually by growing plants that will cover some of the surface), and organisms, added that complete with or eat the algae and green organisms, the algae will be kept to a permissible level. Filters and UV clarifiers, algicides and proprietary preparations are available to help control green water as well as natural systems such as reed filter beds and barley straw.

An electric pump is normally used to force the water to a higher level, so that it returns naturally to its original level over a waterfall. Alternatively, it can be ejected into the air through a fountain nozzle. These methods both cause the water to break up into droplets, which have a large surface area and can pick up more oxygen; this oxygen-enriched water is excellent for supporting pond life.

Above: *A waterfall is an ideal way to increase the oxygen level in the water, helping both fish and plants.*

Avoid making the water too rich in nutrients by feeding the aquatic plants with ordinary fertilizers, manure or humus, as this will encourage the growth of algae; instead, keep to those fertilizers made exclusively for aquatic use.

Another problem that can occur is the draining into the pool of water from surrounding areas of grass and vegetation, bringing with it chemicals that have been used as fertilizers, or for killing pests, diseases or plants. Depending on the nature of these chemicals, the water can cause either temporary or permanent damage. Most modern chemicals are checked for toxicity and are passed for domestic use only if they have been proved perfectly safe when used as instructed. However, old chemical sprays and treatments are still available that can cause pollution in the garden pool. Where possible make sure that any natural drainage into the pond is diverted to drain away in a place where damage will not occur. When using sprays try to ensure that the fine droplets are not carried by the wind into the pond.

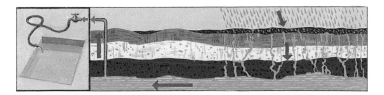

Above: *The mineral content of tap water is determined by the soils that the rain has filtered through.*

Below: *The chemicals emitted by factories can combine with water vapour in the air to form acid rain.*

Pond containers

The pond container is something to hold the water and prevent it from running away or seeping into the surrounding soil. These are available in a variety of materials and shapes, and they can be sunk into the soil to be flush with the soil surface or raised up to form a decorative feature. The cost can vary, depending on the material used and the size. Choosing the material and size will depend very much on your bank balance, your needs and where you wish to put the pond. Ensure that your choice leaves you with a pond that is neither too large for the garden nor too small for the intended fish.

A simple pond will need to have a surface area of at least $1.8m^2$ ($20ft^2$) to support 10 small fishes. Remember that they are going to grow, so that for each 15cm (6in) of fish it is advisable to have $1800cm^2$ ($2ft^2$). To allow not only for the growth of the fishes but also for them to multiply, it is always wise to make a larger pool so that it will cope with its fish population for a number of years. The depth is also important: if it is too shallow, the water will overheat in summer and freeze solid in winter. A deeper pond will allow a wider choice of plants as well as a varied selection of common and exotic fishes.

If you have a formal garden of regular beds and paths, the pond should be rectangular or circular to blend in with the existing arrangement. If, on the other hand, your garden is more natural, with random clumps of planting, meandering paths and a casual layout, then the pond should be as natural as possible, with an irregular shape and looking as if man had no hand in its formation.

With raised ponds where the surface is above ground level, a more formal or regular shape is best; only a rock pool backed by a cliff that cascades its overflow to ground level to be recycled back to the higher pool would look natural. Obviously a raised pond needs a substantial container to prevent the vast weight of water bursting the sides. The advantage of the raised pond is that it allows you to see the fishes and plants and study them closely without stooping.

Below: *Liners to contain water are made either from polythene, PVC which can be reinforced with nylon, or butyl rubber (the most expensive).*

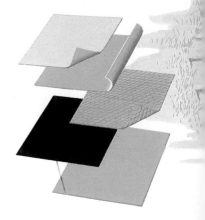

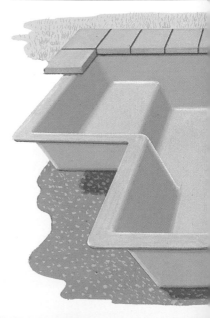

Above: *The liner is stretched across the pool cavity and anchored with* stones. *Water is poured on the liner, which stretches to fill the hole.*

Left: *A precast pool can be set into the ground by excavating a hole for it to sit in and edging it with slabs.*

Above: *Pond containers are available in many sizes, shapes and materials.*

Types of container

The cheapest form of container uses a plastic liner to contain the water in an excavation. This liner is made of polythene, which breaks down when exposed to sunlight, so it must be shaded between the pool edge and the water level. It has an estimated life of just a year or two, and can only be recommended as a temporary structure. Other liners using plastic have a guaranteed life of three years for the plain and ten years for the laminated varieties; the best quality is the liner made from butyl rubber; this is guaranteed for 15 years but has a life expectancy of over 50 years, and should give a lifetime's use without trouble. With a liner, a pond of almost any shape or size can be made, limited only by your purse and the size of your garden.

Concrete is a wet form of construction that is labour intensive and involves the use of shuttering to contain the concrete until it has cured. Concrete is fine where there is a good solid foundation underneath and the water table is not close to the surface, but where there is a chance of movement it can crack; this will allow the water to seep away, and if the crack is very fine it is difficult to trace for repair.

Precast pools are made from plastic in various weights and in fibreglass. The cost varies and, as in most things, you get what you pay for. The cheapest models are thin and vulnerable to damage; the thicker plastic ones are either semi-rigid or rigid and strong, but more costly; and the most expensive are constructed from fibreglass, which should give a lifetime's use. These pools are fine if the shape and size available happens to meet your requirements.

Should the worst occur and your pool start to leak, there are repair kits that will seal the pool, but usually you will have to empty the water out, store the livestock in a separate container, and replace and balance the water before the livestock can be replaced.

Left: *A pond can be built on a foundation slab using bricks or concrete blockwork and made impervious to water seepage by painting the inside with a pond paint or cement rendering.*

Right: *A raised pond can be made with a precast pool shell but it will need to have a strong foundation to stop any tilting and to prevent any distortion of the shell with the weight of water in the finished pond.*

Opposite page: *A raised pool allows fish and water plants to be close to the viewer for examination and appreciation.*

Water movers

Above and left: *Fountains can vary from a small bubble jet to a spray that lifts the water several metres.*

Below: *A non-submersible pump kept in a separate pump house draws the water out of the pond via the pump and returns it to the pool.*

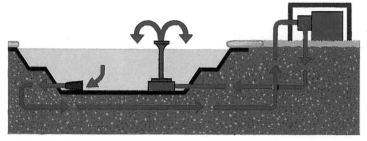

For most gardeners achieving water movement entails some form of power to lift it to a higher level so that gravity draws it back to its original level. This usually takes the form of an electric pump that forces the water through a jet or series of jets to form a fine spray that falls back into the water splashing and extending the water's surface to expose it to as much air as possible. Alternatively, the water is lifted to a higher level so that it can run down through a stream over a waterfall or series of ledges where it can splash and increase the oxygen level. Once it has returned to the pump level it is then pumped up again to repeat the cycle. Apart from the important oxygenating effect, the movement of water is pleasing to eye and ear, particularly on a hot sunny day when it has a cooling effect and will perhaps lay a little dust.

There are more gentle forms of

moving water that are decorative, where a tall fountain is unsuitable. In draughty areas where the spray drift might be a nuisance, a lower and more concentrated form of fountain can be obtained by using a bell-fountain, which gives a thin, dome-shaped curtain of water around the fountain head. Another form of movement can be achieved by pumping the water through the central hole in a millstone so that it bubbles and spreads over the stone surface, then trickles down the sides to be returned to the pump.

Types of water pumps

Pumps come in a variety of sizes and in two types, the submersible and the surface pump. Choose one that is suitable for the amount of water to be moved and the height it has to be lifted. The manufacturers usually give the pump output with the varying

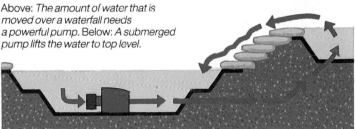

Above: *The amount of water that is moved over a waterfall needs a powerful pump.* Below: *A submerged pump lifts the water to top level.*

heights it can be used, in either litres or gallons. A small pump will provide a gentle flow of water suitable for the small pond, but a bigger pump will need a larger pool to move more water without causing too much turbulence in the pool. A large pump can give a powerful gush of some five times the flow of a smaller pump. The fountain can also vary from a single jet of great power to a cluster of sprays of a more modest height. When choosing, keep in mind the scale of the garden: a small spray would look pathetic in a lake, and a giant geyser would be completely out of scale in a small town garden. For most purposes a medium-sized pump with a flow of some 2-3000 litres (440-660 gallons) per hour is ample to give either a steady flow over a waterfall or a display of fountain jets.

The submersible pump works under water. It has a filter system that

prevents fishes and pool debris from being sucked into the moving parts. The water is forced along a pipe to the outlet. Being under water it has to be completely sealed around the electrical circuit. The water keeps the pump cool, and it is silent in action.

The surface pump is usually much larger and more powerful, and requires a weatherproof pump house. It normally needs priming (filling the pump chamber with water to start the action), is often noisier and costs more. This type of pump is recommended only for very large pools where there is to be a spectacular water display, which is usually to the detriment of ornamental fishes in the pool.

Fountain nozzles are available in a variety of forms and can be fixed to free-standing figures, architectural mouldings or wall-mounted features such as lions' heads or dolphins.

Electricity in the garden

The combination of electricity and water can be lethal, particularly when a human being joins the two together, but if protected properly it is perfectly safe. The first rule is to make sure that all electrical equipment that is bought has been expressly made for outdoor use, and that all instructions, no matter how silly or inappropriate they may seem, are followed to the letter. The second rule is to keep it in good repair and well maintained. Where cables have to be used in the garden – especially if they are to be buried under flower beds – use an armoured cable (one that is covered with toughened plastic or metal). All switches and junction boxes must be completely waterproof.

If in any doubt about your system, call in a qualified electrician to advise you. Secure all cables so that they will not cause any hazard; avoid draping wires along a flimsy fence that could be blown down in a severe gale, and keep them out of hedges or shrubs that are likely to be clipped or pruned. If you decide to run the cable under ground, bury it deeper than 45cm (18in) to prevent a garden spade inadvertently severing it. Also make sure that the cable route is clearly

marked: you might remember where it runs, but if the house is sold the new occupiers need to know where the cable is to avoid trouble. A plastic strip is available to warn of buried cables. All this may sound too much trouble, but it is vitally important.

Safety measures
It is not always necessary to have full mains electricity to run pool equipment. The current can be stepped down through a transformer to a lower AC voltage or to very low DC voltage provided the equipment is suitable. If an accident occurs, the

Above: The enjoyment of the garden can be extended after dark by using electricity to power lights and the pump that moves water in the pool.

shock would then be well within safety limits and cause no harm.

As a safety precaution, all outside main circuits should be fitted with a circuit breaker so that if there is any leakage of current the circuit breaker automatically switches off the power. Choose a model that is suitable for personal protection, rated at 30 milliamps, and takes no more than 30 milliseconds to trip. This will ensure

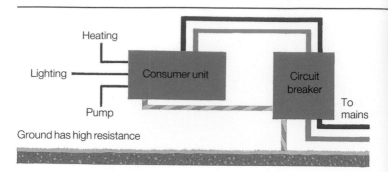

Heating

Lighting

Consumer unit

Circuit breaker

To mains

Pump

Ground has high resistance

Above: *Position the circuit breaker between the consumer unit and the main fuse to give full protection.*

that if someone touches a live wire or a live section of a piece of equipment, then the instant the current starts to run through the person it will switch

Below: *There is a wide variety of lights that are made for outdoor use and are highly suitable for the garden. Some are constructed to work under water with a choice of colour filters. Lights can be permanently fixed or portable, giving spots or general illumination.*

off before any damage is caused and the person will be unharmed. There are various models of circuit breaker; they can be wired into the electrical circuit at the fuse box, or they can be wired in as a power socket or as part of a plug. The plug will cover only one appliance, but the socket, provided it has an adaptor, can service more than one item, and the circuit controller will cover all the machines on the whole circuit.

Lighting and heating
Electricity is not only for pumps but also covers lighting and heating. Here

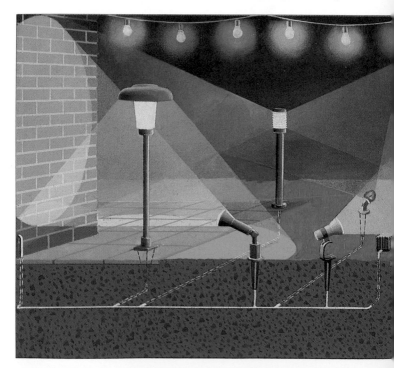

again it is important to use the right equipment – lights that have been designed specially for exterior use, either as individual lights or as strings of bulbs for illuminating the garden. Some lights for the pond are used floating or submerged, sometimes attached to a fountain to give a variety of colours to the spray. Most lighting comes in either flood or spot models: the flood will illuminate a wide area, whereas the spot throws a concentrated beam onto one feature, and gives a more dramatic effect. Where light is required to illuminate a hazard such as steps it is better to use a flood, which has a more overall light, rather than a spot, which can cause confusing shadows.

The low-powered lighting circuits that are available in kits complete with transformer allow the user to clip the lights directly into the cable, which is covered with a self-sealing plastic so that when the light is removed the cable becomes weatherproof again. The light can be placed anywhere along the length of cable without complicated cable stripping.

Where lighting cables are strung overhead it is necessary to support the wire with an additional stout galvanized wire secured to it with clips. Insulating tape is a short-term method that will rot after a year or two, leaving the cable unsupported. Plastic plant ties or clips will last much longer and hold the cable securely. A combination of both tape and ties is even better, as the tape will prevent any chafing.

Electricity provides a very convenient and easy form of power that gives light, drives motors and provides heating – the last is very useful when the pool becomes frozen in winter. Floating a special heater will keep a small area of the pool clear of ice; the fishes will benefit from the oxygen intake, and it will prevent the build-up of noxious gases under the ice. Sophisticated systems can be constructed using a thermostat so that the current is switched on automatically when the temperature drops below freezing and off again when it rises; this cuts down the current used to keep the pond clear.

Using a plastic liner

Place the pond out in the open where possible; this will encourage good plant growth. Allow plenty of space around it for access to the fish and plants. Mark out the area needed and then check the levels; it is very rare to find a garden that is absolutely flat, even if it looks level. The pool structure must lie level and the spoil dug out can be used to build up a ridge to make the liner just contain the water and not stick up at one end.

When digging the pond it is important to incorporate shelves along the sides, at least 20cm (8in) wide and 23cm (9in) below the water surface, to accommodate plants that

need just a little water over their roots. The deeper parts can be dug to a depth suitable for your plants and fishes: this should be not less than 45cm (18in) deep. Deeper ponds are needed for Koi, which need water about 1.5m (5ft) deep. Shallow ponds are prone to freezing in winter and overheating in summer, to the distress of the fishes. Remove a strip of turf around the edge, about 5cm (2in) deep and 45cm (18in) wide, for the liner to bed into.

The liner should be plenty large enough and the size can be calculated by taking the overall dimensions and adding double the

depth to the length and double the depth to the width. For example, if the hole measures 3.6m (12ft) long, 2.4m (8ft) wide and 60cm (2ft) deep, then the liner should be 3.6m (12ft) plus twice the depth of 60cm (2ft) long and 2.4m (8ft) plus twice the depth of 60cm (2ft) wide, so the pool requires a liner 4.8m (16ft) by 3.6m (12ft).

The liner needs to be pulled fairly taut across the pool and anchored round the edge with heavy weights such as paving slabs. Water is then poured into the liner, which will stretch with the weight and start to conform to the profiles of the cavity, becoming more tight to the walls as the water reaches the top. Trim the liner to leave 30-45cm (12-18in) excess to be covered with turf or paving; the latter can be bedded in a layer of mortar. (Treat cement to prevent lime leaching into the pool.)

Below: Mark out the pool shape with pegs and string, check the levels, then start the excavation. Line the hole with a layer of sand to give a smooth surface; then stretch the liner over, anchoring the edges with stones. Next, pour in the water, which stretches the liner to fit the hole's contours. Finally, trim the edges and cover with stones or turf.

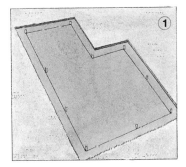

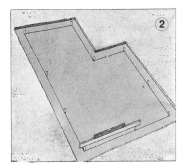

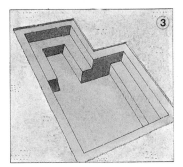

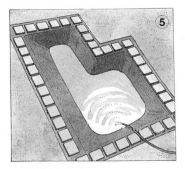

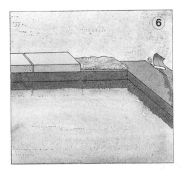

Using a precast shell

Positioning a precast pond is best achieved by inverting the shell and laying it on the ground in the right place and marking its exact outline, but this is unfortunately suitable only for symmetrical pools. Irregular ones have to be placed right way up, and the edge marked by dropping vertical positions to the ground. Check the levels to allow for any building-up of soil around one end, otherwise you may have one end of the precast shell sticking out of the ground.

When a precast pond has to be set into the soil it is necessary to dig a hole to conform as closely to the shell as possible. This is quite an undertaking, particularly if the shell is large, and when the hole is completed there are usually some gaps around the edge that need to be back-filled. This is done with sand, ramming it well down to give the cast as much support as possible. There are difficulties where the gaps are under the planting shelves or the shell's base; but if a layer of sand is spread on these flat surfaces and the cast wriggled into position, the sand will conform closely to the shape of the shell. Awkward areas are sometimes filled with sand by forcing down the sand with a jet of water from a hosepipe, which will wash the sand into the cavities that otherwise cannot be reached.

Once the precast pond is in position and the edges again checked for levels it can be filled with water, which will make it settle a little. A semi-rigid pool cast will have its sides pressed out against the walls of the hole, but the fibreglass models are more rigid and will be more inflexible. Some ponds have the edge built into the cast and can be left exposed, whereas others need a covering to make them a little more unobtrusive. This can be done using turf, stone or paving slabs, though the latter need to be bedded onto a layer of mortar for stability. Remember to leave the water to settle for a reasonable length of time, so that it can reach the temperature of its surroundings and lose the chlorine and other harmful gases. Only then should you set about introducing plants and fishes into the pond.

Above: *A pond similar to this can be constructed using a precast shell. The shell is initially placed upside down in its intended position and*

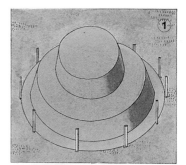

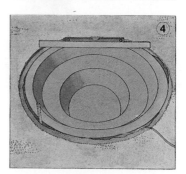

marked with pegs. The hole is then excavated to conform as closely as possible to the shell, which is placed in the hole and any gaps are packed with sand. The levels are checked and the pool filled with water; the edge can be trimmed with paving slabs or stones for a neat effect.

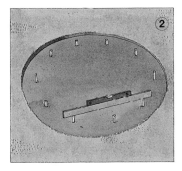

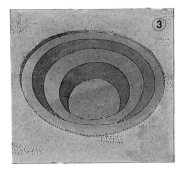

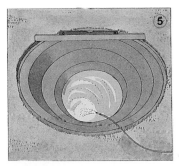

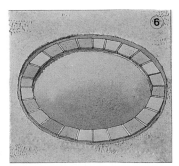

A raised precast pond

A raised pond needs a substantial foundation under the cast to prevent the pond tilting or sinking, and plenty of reserve strength around it to contain the weight and stop the shell distorting and splitting. After placing the shell in position, carefully measure the height of the pond and mark it with canes and string so that you can be satisfied with the overall positioning. Remove the top soil, spread a 10cm (4in) layer of hardcore over the site and firm it down well. Place a further 10cm (4in) of concrete over the top and smooth off.

If the overall dimensions are in excess of 2.4m (8ft) in either direction it is wise to include some steel reinforcing. This can be welded mesh or a grid of rods wired together to form 10-15cm (4-6in) squares. Large ponds should have the thickness of concrete increased to 15cm (6in) to give a stable base, and this thickness

Below: *Place the casting in position and mark off with pegs; remove the top soil and lay a foundation slab on top of hardcore. The shell is then replaced and the perimeter wall is built backfilling with concrete; as this proceeds, the pool is filled with water. Finally, the top is finished with slabs. Allow to settle before planting.*

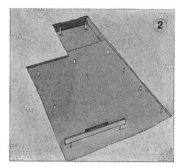

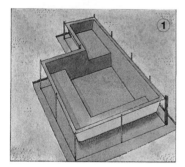

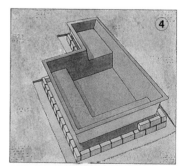

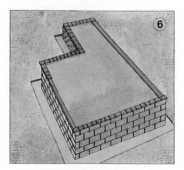

should also be used where the soil is soft or unstable, whatever the size.

The cast can be set onto the concrete if both surfaces are smooth, but if either is irregular then a bed of mortar should be spread for the shell to be vibrated into place; check the levels in both directions. The perimeter wall needs a foundation similar to the pond base, with the hardcore finishing some 45cm (18in) below ground level and 45cm (18in) wide to provide adequate support for a wall of 23cm (9in) thickness.

The wall can be constructed of brick, concrete block or stone to fit into the garden scheme. As it rises a weak mixture of concrete of eight parts of ballast to one of cement can be packed between the wall and the cast; the concrete should be only just moist. If the cast appears too flexible it can be part filled with water to compensate for the exterior pressure.

Continue the wall and back-filling until level with the top of the cast, and smooth off to give a fine finish on the top surface. An alternative is to cover the top with stone or tiles, which should be set into a mortar bed and pointed between the stones or tiles to give a frost-proof finish. The pond should be filled with water and allowed to settle before planting.

Using concrete

Mark out with pegs the area to be covered by the pond. Check the levels with a spirit level to make sure that the whole structure will be set into the ground without any section projecting above the surface; if this is likely to happen, some additional soil should be dug out allowing for the thickness of the walls and base, which depends on the shape, depth and size of the pond. Unless you are constructing the pond in solid rock you should allow at least 10cm (4in) thickness for a small pond and 15cm (6in) for a larger one.

Where possible incorporate some reinforcing material: chicken wire is suitable for small ponds, but larger ones need reinforcing with something more substantial, and the fairly complicated large ponds with several levels really require the services and expertise of a fully qualified structural engineer to work out the stresses. This is very important, for even a small pond can hold several tons of water.

Having excavated the hole, check it again for the levels. Prepare the reinforcing and spread the concrete over the base, adding the reinforcing where necessary. The whole is tamped down, to squeeze out any air bubbles, and then allowed to mature for a day or so. The shuttering for the walls is placed into position; this is substantial boarding to hold the wet and plastic concrete in place until it is dry. The concrete is poured into this mould in one action, vibrated to allow air bubbles to escape, and left to set. The shuttering can then be removed, and the base and walls covered with a slurry of sharp sand and cement rubbed well into the surface and allowed to dry thoroughly.

Once the pond is complete, you will need to treat it with a proprietary liquid plastic seal to prevent lime leaching from the cement into the water. You can then fill the pond with water, treat with a dechlorinator, and, after a few days, start to plant it out and add one or two fish. Other fish should be added in small quantities after a period of months. This will prevent problems later on.

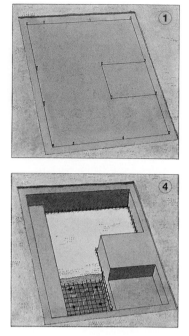

Above: *Mark out the pond position with pegs and string, check the levels, and then dig out the hole. To lay a suitable concrete foundation slab*

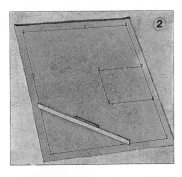

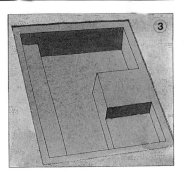

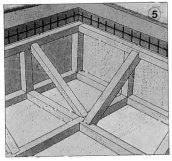

incorporating some reinforcing metal, put up some shuttering to hold the wet concrete sides in position; place in the reinforcement before pouring and vibrating the concrete. Remove the shuttering when the concrete is dry and paint the sides with a pool paint to contain the chemicals.

Small formal ponds

If a small garden of some 12m (40ft) square is to contain a pond and a formal arrangement, it needs careful planning. The formal shape requires a pattern that can be either symmetrical or not, but usually incorporating straight lines and regular curves in the layout. It can be classical in concept, like part of a Grecian temple, or just an arrangement of definite squares, rectangles, circles or half-circles of paving, planting or areas of water, put together to provide a complete scene to suit your taste.

With such a small area and usually with restricted access it is wise to forgo a lawn and use paving instead. With the variety of different types and colours available now, there is no need for an area of paving to look boring; it can be divided up into sections of contrasting colour or shape to give variety.

The pond can be simple or dramatic, sunk below ground level or raised up, with fountains or waterfalls to provide movement of water that is in scale with the size of the garden, and room for a few choice aquatic plants and a small selection of fancy fishes. Constructions around the pond must harmonize with the garden style: simple paving-slab bridges and stepping stones fit into a formal scheme far better than their rustic counterparts, and planting in the garden needs to be fairly ordered and regular in shape and type. Conifers in pots will not drop their leaves in autumn, yet will give height and foliage colour all the year round. Bright colours can be provided by using bulbs for spring blooms and annuals for summer and autumn brilliance, leaving the evergreens to carry their foliage through the winter until spring returns again.

Where there is a change in the level of the site it should be emphasized with steps and walls constructed in a material that links with other garden constructions and with the bricks or stone of the house, in order to keep the formal look to the garden.

Left: *An angular, L-shaped pool with straight edges and regular paving makes a very formal area only softened by the plants and the movement and splash of the water. On the opposite page the hard lines have been muted by the foliage.*

Right: *Use a bare wall to make a water feature by building up two semicircular pools and a wall-mounted fountain. Evergreens are used to provide an all-year-round background without the autumn problem of leaves, and placed to give a near symmetrical design.*

Small informal ponds

Ponds of informal design need to look very natural, as if they have just been picked up from the wild and dropped into the garden. This can be quite difficult to achieve in a garden that is only some 12m (40ft) square. One important factor is to ensure that the pond does not overpower the rest of the garden by its size, nor should it be too small and tucked away in a corner. The surface reserved for sitting and walking on should look natural and casual, with the use of as much natural material as possible. If it is necessary to use regular precast paving, then use it in a random fashion to avoid any feeling of formality. Gravel, sections cut from tree trunks and random pieces of stone can be used, separately or mixed, to give an informal air to the garden and the pond surround.

The pond can have a curved irregular shape, but keep it simple to avoid pockets of water becoming stagnant. Waterfalls also need to look as natural as possible. Constructions in the pond can be quite rustic in feeling; use wood to make bridges, and large lumps of rock or boulders to form edges and provide cascades for the water to tumble down.

Another way to keep a natural look and avoid the tailored effect of mown grass is to make an irregular shape close to the water that is close cut, but leave a surrounding section to grow higher; this will soften the appearance and help to keep a pleasant informal arrangement. Planting also needs to be kept looking informal, with tufts of plants and casual clumps of shrubs and trees. Try to keep to evergreens to avoid the leaf problem in autumn. Flowers look happiest if they are dotted casually around the garden in a disordered way, like a meadow of wild flowers.

Slopes or irregularities in the soil levels can be used to advantage to make mounds and small outcrops of stone, to emphasize the natural feel of the garden. The spoil from the pond excavation can be used to good effect by building up a small hillock, and this gives some height to what may be an otherwise flat garden site. Do not let water drain from such a new rise into the pond, though.

Above: *An informal look is achieved by keeping the curves natural and the planting simple and well positioned without overcrowding.*

Left: *In a simple design the spoil from the pool is used to make a mound covered with rocks for a waterfall; the lack of straight edges helps to give a casual look.*

Far left: *An ambitious design with a bridge to the raised section, sheltered with evergreen planting and keeping a suitably natural feel with the irregular arrangement of the paving.*

Small semi-formal ponds

Right: *A sloping site is used to make a stepped arrangement, allowing water and two styles of paving to break up a hard area; planting may be restricted to forming a background.*

Far right: *With hexagonal paving an irregular edge is given to the pool; stepping stones and a fountain also make the design less rigid. The bare wall has been covered with a creeper.*

The semi-formal garden often has the best of both the formal and the informal world. When used well the mixture of natural arrangement and ordered constructions can be most effective. It is less hard-looking than the formal garden and yet is not wild enough to be classed as informal, having the appearance of a piece of man-made construction surrounded by nature; this echoes the house structure surrounded by or neighboured by nature in the garden.

Paving may be regular or irregular in shape, man-made or natural. Walls can be brick, stone or timber, and the planting may take the form of either natural disorder or a more restricting order. But whatever style is followed it is important to strike a balance. To design this semi-formal type of garden in a small 12m (40ft) square takes some skill, but keep the pond shape simple, with either a fountain or a waterfall (of formal or informal concept, whether a natural cascade or a concrete structure) to give movement to the water.

Pond constructions can use a variety of materials: wood, stone, concrete or brick. It is wise to relate some of the materials to the house so that there is some connection between the two, whether it is bricks or stone that make the transition.

Plants can be neatly confined to containers, left to ramble along a boundary, or even grouped into irregular clumps. Planting in the water should allow the leaf and flower shapes to be seen clearly as well as the fishes in the water, which can be either fancy or not, according to the owner's tastes. Choose evergreens where possible, to avoid leaves falling into the pond during autumn. Provide colour by growing annuals, perennials, bulbs, shrubs and flowering trees, to give some interest throughout the year. In a garden of this size, the inclusion of a number of heavily scented flowers can give particular delight during the spring and summer months.

Left: *The mixture of formal and informal styles can be most attractive, keeping the advantages of simple shapes with a natural look.*

41

Medium-sized formal ponds

A medium-sized garden can incorporate a larger pond and a more complex system of moving water involving streams and waterfalls. This type of design can happily form part of a larger garden, and here the design is concentrated in a squarish section that contains the water garden some 18m (60ft) square.

The use of regular geometric shapes helps to give formality to the design, whether it is a series of interlocking squares and rectangles, circles or a simple symmetrical shape. The water element can be raised above the ground to form a dramatic tower system gushing water; a low container that allows one to sit upon the edge; or even a below-ground-level construction that is meant to be viewed from above.

The use of different materials will help to provide visual interest. Railway sleepers set into gravel, paving mixed with brick, concrete with stone chips, or reconstituted stone with natural stone, can all give variety of texture and colour to set off the sparkle of water. Pond construction can be made of the same materials or contrasting with a random pile of natural rocks. Water can be moved through fountains or over waterfalls using different forms to give a dramatic or interesting effect to the overall design.

Low-growing plants can soften hard paving or gravel; tall trees give instant height if bought as container plants or as specimens several years old; tubs of plants can be moved from one place to another to give variety whenever the owner chooses; and climbers trained up trellis or large plain walls can screen out unwanted views and provide a measure of privacy. Annuals, perennials, bulbs and shrubs will give a brilliant display in spring, summer and autumn, leaving the evergreens to continue through the winter (with their different shapes and wide variety of hues of green, yellow, blue and red foliage).

The cost of such a pond can vary considerably, depending on the materials and the amount used, but by choosing wisely you can make an exciting pond setting without too much strain on the purse.

Below: *A formal double circular pool with the jungle air of a thatched summerhouse and bamboos.*

Above: *The careful use of old railway sleepers and brick paving makes this design unusual and interesting.*

Below: *A very formal arrangement sees the plants carefully matched and placed in a regular pattern.*

Medium-sized informal ponds

The opportunities offered by having a medium-sized area of about 18m (60ft) square in which to design an informal pond are many. The main aim is to look as if a slice or section of nature has been lifted out and placed in your garden. This entails great care in the placing of the various elements that will make up the area. The shapes, particularly that of the pond, need to be casual in appearance and as un-manmade as possible.

For a special effect, the human touch can give a dramatic gesture, like a marble statue set in a natural-looking grotto. Use natural materials, and avoid concrete and regular patterns, especially for seating areas; use timber, stone, gravel and grass. The timber needs to be discrete, not raw, freshly sawn timber that stands out like a sore thumb; treat new wood with a preservative that is dull in

colour, to make it blend into the overall design of the pond area.

Pond shapes should be curved, and the curves need to be gentle, as if worn with time. Keep any straight lines to constructions such as bridges, piers or landing stages. Large pieces of stone should be used in construction work as this helps give the garden a sense of scale. Large logs of timber will give the feeling of strength; and islands need to be big enough to sit on, or to grow a specimen tree for shade.

Planting should look casual and without order, some close together and others wide apart. Use the more natural plants to form clumps and groups, instead of exotic-looking specimens placed obviously at a focal point. The use of evergreens will cut down problems with the autumn leaf fall, and colour can be provided by

using bulbs, annuals, perennials, flowering shrubs and trees.

Use any slope or variation in the levels to advantage, to make a more dramatic effect with mounds, banks and hollows or (with the use of stone) to make an outcrop of rock or a scree area. The spoil from the pond excavation can be used to build up a hillock for a cascade.

Above: *Under the riot of colourful plants there is a careful design contriving to give a natural appearance to the water and stone.*

Below: *A free-form pool that has an island coupled to the garden by a wooden bridge screened with casual evergreen planting gives this garden a natural and pleasing appearance.*

Medium-sized semi-formal ponds

Above: *A fine mixture of formal and informal elements make this a very pleasant garden.*

Left: *A simple design involving a paved area round a regular shaped pool next to a beach, with a planting of evergreens to give a natural background.*

Right: *A stone figure in a small pool and flanked with mirrors can give the illusion of more space.*

To design a medium-sized garden with a water feature in a semi-formal manner will mean mixing elements that can look opposed in style. This can succeed if there is a balance: for example, a formal element can be treated as an extension of the existing formality of the house structure, and a terrace, deck area, patio or sitting space can use regular shapes and obviously man-made materials that echo those used in the house construction. This major element can then blend into or be placed next to an informal pond or planting space, where one can step from a rectangular area designed for entertaining onto gravel or pebbles laid in a random manner next to a curved stretch of water that contains a formal fountain and is surrounded by a mixture of wild and specimen planting. This mixture needs care and skill so that it does not look too confusing with everything vying for attention. The more dominant areas need playing down. With the right use of materials, such as timber and stone, the garden will look more relaxed and harmonious.

Pond shapes can be curved or straight, and edged with grass, paving or random boulders intermingled with pebbles, with water moving through fountains or waterfalls or a combination of both. Decks overlapping the pond can be used for barbecues, for sunbathing, or even as a site for a Jacuzzi. Constructions need to be in scale with the garden; avoid anything that is going to make the space look poky. It is better to have one large object – whether it is a rock, a statue, a water feature or a tree – rather than a collection of little ones.

Planting should be arranged to give interest in groups and variety in heights. There are plenty of trees with different forms that are evergreen, even a weeping cedar, which makes a fine feature by water, far superior to the popular weeping willow, which drops its leaves, and undermines the pond and any other building nearby with its roots. Use any natural slopes of the site or variations in level to make the garden and pool surround more sculptural and exciting.

Constructions in the pond

There are obvious objects that can be constructed in the garden pond, such as islands and bridges; but there are also less obvious items such as decks, jetties, stepping stones, waterfalls, and bases for sculpture and fountains that border or intrude into the water area. These can be a problem when it comes to placing them into position. The most important problem is how to put them into place without upsetting, breaking or damaging the pond structure, whether it is concrete, plastic liner or a precast shell. If there is an adequate concrete base under the pond, there should be no problem; and of course it is better to think of this element before the pond is constructed, in order to make allowances in the foundation work, and add extra strength where there is to be extra weight. But if you inherit a pond or have a sudden desire to add to your own construction, it will entail certain precautions for success.

The best method, when you have a heavy weight that has to rest on something rather fragile, is to spread the load over a wide area; this means making the foundation cover as wide a space as possible. If you have a pond liner and you wish to build a pier to support a bridge, fountain or stepping stone, place a large flat stone (or even a couple of paving slabs) on the flat base of the pond to carry the weight. If the slab has sharp edges and corners these should be cushioned with a double layer of pond liner – a piece of the original liner that was trimmed off when it was being constructed will be sufficient. Upon this flat slab the structure can be built up with confidence.

If the pond is in use, remember that any cement or concrete work will give off free lime into the water, which can damage the livestock. All work should be treated with a suitable pond paint to isolate new cement work. To keep structures as light as possible, use hollow blocks and build with plenty of holes in the construction.

Where there is an undulating base that does not allow a paving slab to bed flat on the base, a layer of sand can fill out the hollows and give the slab something to setle down on. This

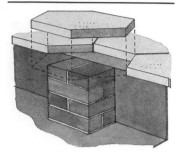

Above: *It is necessary to build a pier to support a hexagonal paving slab that projects over the pool edge.*

Below: *Stepping stones can be made on top of a pool liner by spreading the weight over a larger area using paving slabs. All concrete materials have to be painted with pond paint to seal in the chemicals. Hollow blocks can be filled using plastic bags of concrete.*

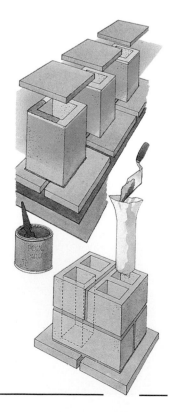

Above: A bridge adds beauty to this pool.

Left: When building a pier or jetty on a sloping base it is necessary to provide a concrete foundation under the liner to support the weight evenly.

Right: When using timber poles for constructions, they can be either fixed with nails, screws or bolts, or wired together using heavy duty staples into the main timbers.

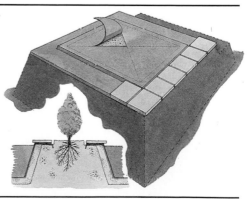

Right: An island can be made in a pool even when using a liner. It should be distinguished as a shape in the excavation, so the liner is stretched over it when filled with water. The edge of the island is secured with slabs and the plastic cut to expose the soil which can then be planted.

will not work on a sloping base, where it is usually necessary to build up a foundation of wet concrete; this invariably means draining the pond to make a good job.

Constructing an island is a simple matter when the pond is originally being built with a liner; leave the soil in position and stretch the liner over it, anchor it and trim the edges as the ordinary pond edge. Where there is an existing pond, it is best to build a wall of brick or stone and infill with soil to make an island.

Timber can be used, but make sure that any wood preservative that has been used is suitable for the pond and livestock. If the timber has weathered well it can be used, but if in doubt cover the timber in a seal such as yacht varnish and allow it to dry thoroughly before placing it in the water. Bridges need to be safe: it is no pleasure to be suddenly dropped into cold water, either by the collapse of the structure or by slipping on a mossy surface. Check that there is adequate strength in the structure, as people like to congregate on a bridge to look at the water and livestock. Railings need to be more than adequate and securely fixed to the whole structure.

Waterfalls and cascades should be built so that no water can escape through leaks, particularly where there are overlaps in the construction. Liners work very well in this sort of structure, being discrete in appearance yet thoroughly reliable.

Below: *To place a pump in shallow water it is necessary to construct a sump to conceal it; the cover can be made from loose-laid paving slabs.*

Below: *When using railway sleepers as pool sides it is important to lay the pool liner behind them to render the whole structure waterproof.*

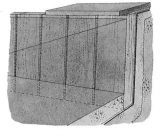

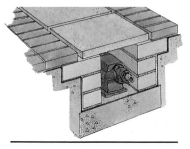

Left and below: *When constructing waterfalls it is important to keep the whole stream contained in a waterproof channel, making sure that liners are used effectively and no leakage occurs. Conceal all piping behind the stonework or planting.*

Above: *An edging of pebbles in a pond can look very sympathetic.*

Right: *When constructing a beach of pebbles it is necessary to provide a container to stop them from rolling down to a lower level. This is achieved by building a raised, rigid section under the pool liner.*

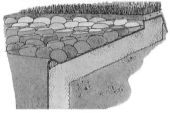

Below: *The use of an old pump head can be most effective as a fountain head, seen here secured to an old railway sleeper as a support.*

Below: *The pump lies below the water surface, where it forces the water up to issue from the pump, and to drop back down and be recycled again.*

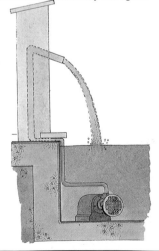

Oxygenating plants

Oxygenating plants provide shelter for spawning fish and their fry, as well as releasing oxygen directly into the water in strong light. They also take up mineral salts from the water that would normally encourage the growth of algae. A dozen or so should be planted in a small container and allow one container to every 2m² (22ft²) in a small pool, but as the pool enlarges relatively fewer containers are needed; a pool of over 55m² (586ft²) would require twenty containers. If the plants become too prolific it is a simple matter to lift out a few containers to allow more space. The following is a selection of useful oxygenating plants.

Elodea canadensis (1)
Canadian Pond Weed; Water Thyme
This plant originates in North America and has dark green, small thyme-like leaves with fine serrations. It increases mainly by the slender and brittle stems rooting at each whorl of leaves. Provided it is pruned of all dead growth it should never die. Keep it in a container to prevent it spreading unduly. *E.callitrichoides* is a finer and more delicate variety.

Fontinalis antipyretica (2)
Willow Moss
Forms dark green clumps and prefers to root in gravel, pebbles and stonework; it is best seen in moving water. The new shoots send out light green buds on the ends of the stems, which are mossy in appearance and harbour many varieties of animal life.

Hottonia palustris (3)
Water Violet; Featherfoil
The plant has feathery bright green leaves under water; only the flower stem rises above the surface and bears pale lilac blooms. It should be

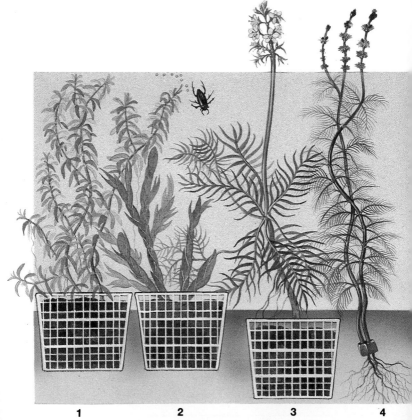

1   2   3   4

planted separately with a piece of the creeping root attached. In autumn the plant forms winter buds that sink into the pool floor to reappear in the spring. The American form *H.inflata* has white flowers.

Lagarosiphon major (syn. Elodea crispa)
A very good oxygenator with curly leaves on long training stems.

Myriophyllum (4)
Milfoil
The delicate feathery leaves are characteristic of this group of plants; most will grow under water and give good service as oxygenators. They are very decorative. A portion of the plant can be weighted and sunk into the pool, where it will quickly root and grow. *M. alterniflorum, spicatum,* and *verticillatum* are all good species to grow and are widely available.

Potamogeton crispus (6)
Curly Pondweed
This plant has long wiry stems with wavy-edged leaves of a shiny brown that give it the appearance of seaweed. It enhances the look of most ponds and is ideal in moving water; plant in clumps near the pump or at the base of a waterfall.

Rorippa nasturtium aquaticum (5)
Water Cress
This plant grows wild in the Northern Hemisphere and is well known for its culinary uses. Plant cuttings directly into containers of fine soil in shallow water and trim it regularly to keep it looking neat. A good oxygenator.

Crassula (Tillaea) recurva (7)
An Australian plant of creeping habit that grows well either submerged or at the water margin. It has very fine stems and leaves with tiny flowers.

5   6   7

Deep water and marginal plants

There are many aquatic plants that grow in deep water. Their roots need soil and this is best kept in a container, allowing the plant to be lifted out of the water for pruning, treating for pests and diseases and for feeding. The container can be a box, pot, basket or a proprietary plastic container. The soil should be plain with the addition of bonemeal; some charcoal lumps will help to keep the soil sweet.

Some plants float on the surface with trailing roots that pick up nutrients from the water and these can be easily lifted out and thinned if they spread too far.

Marginal plants in the main have their rootstocks just under the water with their leaves and flowers held well above the surface. Here again, containers should be used to allow the plant to be lifted out, thinned and stopped from taking over the pond. Many aquatic plants are invasive.

Acorus (1, 2)
Sweet Flag
A group of plants of which *A. calamus* (1), which comes from wide areas in the Northern Hemisphere, and *A. gramineus* (2) from Japan are the two most popular. *A. calamus* has sword-shaped leaves like an iris and flowers that are densely packed on short spurs more like an arum. It reaches a height of about 60-75cm (24-30in). *A. gramineus* is finer with narrow leaves and reaches only 20-30cm (8-12in) tall. A variegated variety is available.

Alisma (3)
Water Plantain
Two varieties are grown as aquatics, *A. lanceolatum* and *A. plantago-aquatica*. These similar plants both originate in the Northern Hemisphere and grow to 15-30cm (6-12in) tall. Spikes of small pink flowers rise above the oval leaves. This plant is quick to establish in the pond.

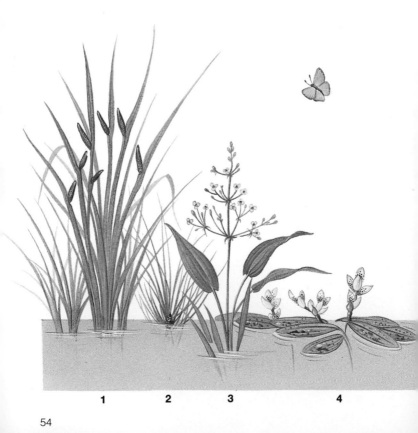

1   2   3   4

Aponogeton distachyos (4)
Water Hawthorn
This South African plant is very decorative, with oblong floating leaves and spikes of scented flowers that rise above the water surface. *A. distachyos* is the hardiest of the family and flowers from early spring to late autumn. This adaptable plant can be grown from tubers or from seed and will thrive in very shallow water or as deep as 45cm (18in).

Azolla (6)
Fairy Moss
Azolla caroliniana and *A. Filiculoides* are two very similar plants native to South America. They are floating plants that form mats of fine fronds on the surface, with the roots taking nourishment from the water. The leaves turn from a fresh green in summer to reddish autumnal tints. In severe climates they are best over-wintered in a pan and kept frost-free.

Butomus umbellatus (5)
Flowering Rush
Native to Europe and Asia, this plant is equally at home in marshland, shallow or deep water. It has long thin green leaves, triangular in section, and bears up to 30 pink or purple flowers in each flowerhead that arise like inverted umbrellas from early summer to early autumn. The plant can reach 1.2m (4ft) tall.

Calla palustris (7)
Bog Arum
Found in the wild in North America, Northern Europe and Asia, this plant has dark green heart-shaped leaves and a creeping rootstock that grows happily in and out of the water. It can be propagated by dividing the roots into sections. The white flowers resemble those of the Arum Lily. After pollination by pond snails, the female flowers mature to red berries. It grows to about 15-20cm (6-8in) in height.

5 6 7

Caltha (1)
Kingcup; Marsh Marigold
Native to North America and Europe, these plants have round serrated leaves and buttercup-like flowers of a golden yellow. The single forms can be grown from seed or root division. Varieties to look for are *C. alba* (white), *C. palustris, C. polypetala* and the double form *C. palustris plena*. They grow in shallow water or wet mud and vary in height from 20cm (8in) to 90cm (3ft), depending on variety.

Carex (2)
Sedge
These perennials from Europe are grass-like and most are very invasive; they should be contained to prevent their spreading. *C. riparia* 'Bowles' Golden', with golden leaves and brown flowers, is recommended as being the least invasive of the genus. It grows to over 30cm (12in) tall.

Cyperus (3)
Umbrella Grass
From Chile and Europe, these sedge-like plants bear clumps of green or brown flowers arranged on stems like an umbrella. *C. eragrostis* is normally hardy and about 60cm (2ft) tall while *C. longus* is hardier but very invasive, reaching up to 1.2m (4ft) in height. The dark green stems of *C. longus* provide excellent cut material for use in flower arrangements. They should not be grown in deep water.

Baldellia (Echinodorus) (4)
These plants from North America and Europe have oval leaves on long stems and bur-like heads; these should be removed to prevent seeding. Flowers are white or pinkish white. *B. ranunculoides* grows up to 45cm (18in), *B. radicans* (not hardy in severe climates) to 1.2m (4ft), and *B. rostratus* (Burhead) to 30cm (12in).

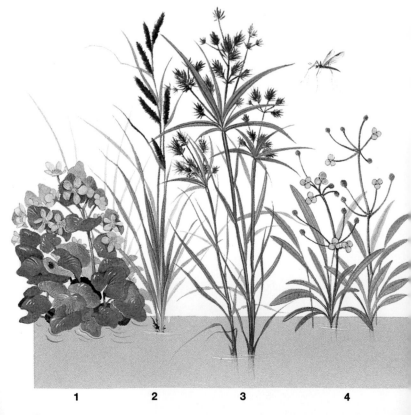

1   2   3   4

Eichhornia crassipes (5)
Water Hyacinth
A prolific species from the tropics, this plant is suited to areas subject to frost as this kills the plant before it can become too invasive. Roots should be lifted and kept just moist from early autumn to late spring and then floated again in the pond during the summer. The leaves are heart shaped and the lilac flowers, borne on spikes up to 38cm (15in) high, are spectacular. The plant spreads to 45cm (18in) wide in one season.

Eriophorum (6)
Bog Cotton; Cotton Grass
A wild plant in the Northern Hemisphere, this genus has grass-like leaves and cotton-like seedheads. *E. angustifolium* grows to 30cm (12in) tall, *E. latifolium* to 45cm (18in) and *E. vaginatum* barely reaches 30cm (12in). All thrive in shallow water or wet mud and can be grown from seed or by root division.

Glyceria aquatica variegata (7)
Manna Grass
A European plant with grass-like leaves arranged in clumps and striped in white, yellow and green with a pink hue in spring and autumn. It will reach 90cm (3ft) if unrestricted but will be only a third of this height if it is grown in a smallish container. Propagate from side shoots.

Houttuynia cordata (8)
From the mountainous regions of the Himalayas through to Japan, this attractive plant has heart-shaped, blue-green leaves, red stems and white flowers with a large central cone. It grows in shallow water and will reach 45-50cm (18-20in) tall. Increase by root division. A double form, *H.c. plena*, is available.

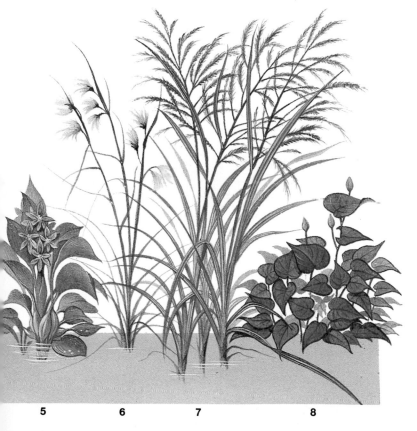

5　　　　**6**　　　　**7**　　　　　　**8**

Hydrocharis morsus-ranae (1)
Frogbit

A floating plant from Europe with bright green, fleshy, kidney-shaped leaves and small white flowers with three petals. Snails and water beetles enjoy the foliage. Terminal buds drop to the bottom of the pond in the autumn and sprout in the following spring; the rest of the plant decays.

Hypericum elodes (2)
Marsh Hypericum

A European plant up to 30cm (12in) tall that makes a good marginal specimen. It has dense rounded foliage and creeping stems covered with fine downy hair. The flowers are yellow and appear in late summer. Increase by dividing the roots.

Iris (3)
Iris; Yellow Flag

A large family of plants with members from many parts of the world: a few thrive in wet conditions. *I. kaempferi* enjoys summer wetness but needs to be dry during the winter; it is best grown in a container that can be removed from the water on to dry land in the autumn and replaced in the spring. The flowers appear in midsummer on stems up to 90cm (3ft) tall. Many varieties are available with single or double blooms in shades of blue, lavender, purple, pink and white. The 'Higo' strain is particularly beautiful. *I. laevigata* enjoys water all the year, producing blue or white flowers. *I. pseudacorus* revels in water up to 45cm (18in) deep, bearing superb yellow flowers on stems up to 1.5m (5ft) high in early summer. *I.p.* 'Variegata' has yellow flowers and yellow-striped foliage. *I. versicolor,* an American plant, produces violet-blue blooms in early summer on 60cm (24in) stems. The lovely variety 'Kermesina' has wine-red flowers in early summer. All these irises can be increased by dividing the rhizome after flowering.

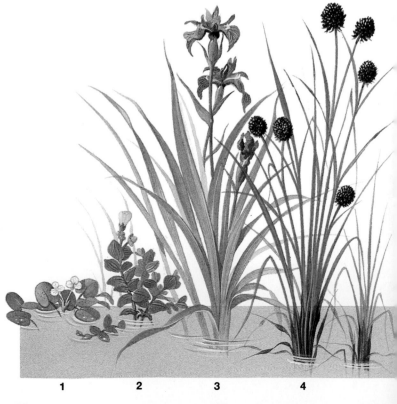

1   2   3   4

Juncus (4)
Rush
A large family spread throughout the world, but only a few species are recommended for the garden pond as they are invasive; all have grass-like leaves. *J. bufonis* has reddish flowers and grows to 20cm (8in) tall. *J. offusus* var. *spiralis* (4) has curious spiral green stems reaching 45cm (18in) in height and *J. ensifolius* has dark brown to blackish flowerheads held 30cm (12in) high. All enjoy either shallow water or moist soil. Be sure to avoid the invasive species.

Mentha aquatica (5)
Water Mint
A European plant with both bright green and brown aromatic leaves, that grows well in either moist soil or shallow water. The lavender blue flowers are borne in clusters. It normally grows to 30cm (12in) tall, but in rich soil it can reach 1m (3.3ft). Increase by division of roots.

Menyanthus trifoliata (6)
Bog Bean; Buck Bean
A Northern Hemisphere plant with light green trifoliate leaves and spikes of rosy white flowers in early summer. It spreads by means of a horizontal rootstock, which makes it suitable for covering pond edges; it grows only about 30cm (12in) tall. Keep this plant constricted and cut it back if it is too vigorous for its chosen site.

Mimulus (7)
Monkey Flower; Monkey Musk
A group of annuals and perennials, mostly from North America; they flower in late summer with red, yellow and orange blooms. *M. guttatus* grows to 45cm (18in) tall with single yellow flowers blotched with crimson. The 'hose-in-hose' varieties have semi-double flowers. *M. cupreus*, *M. lewisii*, *M. maculosus*, *M. moschatus*, *M. ringens* and *M. tigrinus* are all worth growing. They vary in height from 20cm (8in) to 90cm (3ft).

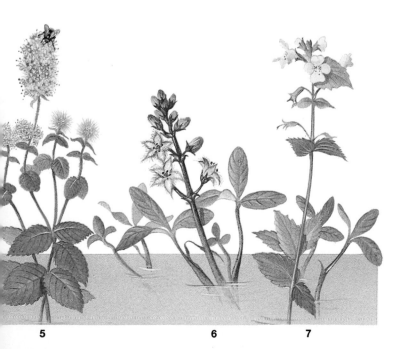

5   6   7

Miscanthus sacchariflorus
Hardy Sugar Cane
This American plant, up to 1.8m (6ft) tall, has the appearance of an ornamental grass and bears flowers noted for the groups of silky hairs at their bases. *M.s. variegata* has white and green variegated foliage.

Myosotis scorpioides (3)
Water Forget-Me-Not
A plant from Europe with many historical and legendary associations. It is ideal for the pool edge, reaching 20cm (8in) tall and bearing bright blue flowers. It seeds well and thrives even in the shade. An improved version, 'Mermaid', has larger and brighter blue flowers. An excellent choice.

Nuphar (1)
Yellow Water Lily; Spatterdock
These water lily-like plants from North America, Europe and Japan have both submerged and floating leaves; the submerged ones are finely divided, the floating ones oval and leathery. The plants have a creeping rootstock and bear yellow dlowers from late spring to early autumn. All grow well in deep and shady water. Some varieties are very vigorous and should be controlled by using containers. For small ponds choose the free-flowering *Nuphar minima*.

Nymphoides peltata (Villarsia nymphoides; Limnanthemum peltatum) (2)
Floating Heart; Water Fringe
A lily-like aquatic plant with rounded floating bright green leaves with crinkled edges. The flowers are yellow, blooming in later summer and held just above the water surface. It will grow well in either deep or shallow water and should be kept in a container to curb its invasive nature.

Orontium aquaticum (4)
Golden Club
A North American plant with strap-shaped floating leaves in deep water; in shallow water the leaves stand up to 45cm (18in) above the surface. They are dark blue-green on the

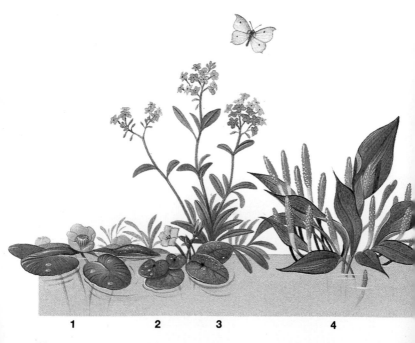

1   2   3   4

upper surface and silver on the undersides. The flowers appear in spring and early summer, yellow in colour and borne on conspicuous white stems. Grow from seed in shallow water and then transplant to deeper water or to soil.

Peltandra
Arrow Arum
There are two North American species, *P. alba* and *P. virginica*. The former has arrow-shaped leaves and white arum-like flowers followed by red berries; the latter has green flowers and green berries. Both grow up to 75cm (30in) in height and can be increased by dividing the rootstock.

Pontederia cordata (5)
Pickerel Weed
A marshland plant from North America, *P. cordata* has shiny heart-shaped deep green leaves and bears blue flowers in late summer. The plant will make large clumps, but they are easily split for smaller areas. It grows up to a height of about 60cm (2ft). A

less hardy species, *P. lanceolata*, has longer lance-like leaves and can reach 1.5m (5ft) in height.

Ranunculus lingua grandiflora (6)
Spearwort
An improved form of a European plant, with narrow leaves and large yellow flowers similar to those of the buttercup; these appear in late spring and summer. It grows to a height of 90cm (3ft) and can be increased by dividing the rootstock. The stems are thick and deep pink in colour. Contain the roots to stop the plant spreading too far and taking over the pond.

Sagittaria (7)
Arrowhead
These plants from Europe and Asia are not generally recommended for a small pond; *S. sagittifolia* and *S. japonica flore pleno* are the two that are suitable; the former needs a container to prevent it spreading. They have distinctive arrow-shaped leaves and white flowers in midsummer. Up to 45cm (18in).

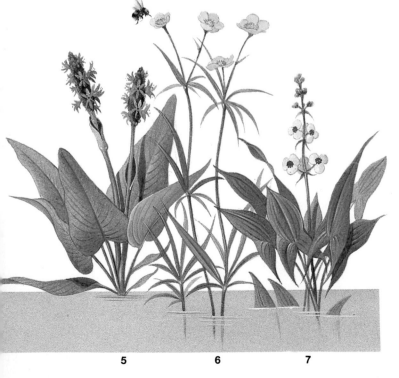

5   6   7

Saururus (1)
Lizard's Tail
From North America comes *Saururus cernuus* and from China and Japan, *S. chinensis*. These plants have dark green heart-shaped leaves and sprays of scented flowers in summer; the former white, the latter cream. Both can reach 45cm (18in) tall.

Schoenoplectus (Scirpus)
Apart from two varieties, these plants should not be used as they are too invasive. Even these two should have their roots contained to prevent them from being too vigorous in growth. *S. lacustris tabernae montani* 'Albescens' has white variegations on the narrow green leaves; it will reach 1.2m (4ft) tall. 'Zebrinus' (Porcupine Quill Rush; Zebra Rush) has green and white bands on the stems and grows to 90cm (3ft) high. Increase both by root division in the spring.

Stratiotes aloides (3)
Water Soldier
A floating plant, found wild in Europe, with sword-like leaves radiating from a central crown. The flowers are small and white; after flowering the plants sink under the surface and produce side shoots that lie dormant until the following spring. Water Soldiers grow to 30cm (1ft) across and prefer alkaline water.

Thalia dealbata (4)
Water Canna
A North American plant with spear-shaped leaves and long spikes of deep purple flowers. In mild areas it can be left to overwinter in the pond, but it requires protection from frost. If in doubt, lift the plants and keep them under cover until late spring. It can grow to 1.8m (6ft) tall in good conditions and can be increased by dividing the rootstock.

1   2   3   4

Trapa natans (5)
Water Chestnut
This annual floating plant from southern Europe has triangular serrated leaves of a bright glossy green. The flowers are small and white and the black seeds (nuts) are large with four spines, and edible. They can be left to ripen on the plant and germinated the following spring.

Typha (6)
Reedmace
These European plants are commonly and erroneously called bulrushes because they have tall grass-like leaves and distinctive brown heads of flowers. They are very invasive and only two are suitable for the garden pond: *T. angustifolia*, which reaches 1.2m (4ft) high, and *T. minima*, which is smaller in scale and only grows to 45cm (18in) tall. Increase both by root division.

Villarsia nymphoides (7)
Floating Heart; Water Fringe
This plant is described under its alternative name of *Nymphoides peltata* on page 60.

Zantedeschia aethiopica (8)
Arum Lily; Lily of the Nile
From Africa, this plant has glossy green leaves and spectacular white flowers during the summer months. It grows up to 90cm (3ft) in height. The true flowers are tiny and yellow, and massed on a central column, or spadix, which is partially enclosed by a showy white modified leaf called a spathe. The plant needs some protection from winter frosts, although hardy varieties are being introduced. One of these is 'Crowborough'. Provide plenty of water during the growing season in spring and summer and increase by dividing the rootstock.

5　　　**6**　　　**7**　　　　**8**

Water lilies

The water lily is justifiably the most popular of water plants. It has brilliant blooms and at the same time its leaves cover the water surface to provide both shelter to fishes and welcome shade that prevents excessive algae growth. In addition, water lilies – all species and hybrids of *Nymphaea* – are available in a variety of sizes to suit the size and depth of any pond, from the pygmy types that need just a shallow covering of water to the more vigorous types that would swamp a small pond completely and need deep water to prevent the leaves from standing proud of the surface.

Water lilies should be grown in containers. They will give sufficient anchorage and nutrition while stopping the plant from outgrowing the pond. They will also allow easy access to the plant for maintenance, treatment for disease or pest attack, and feeding. Containers allow a certain flexibility of position and can be adjusted to give the right depth of water over the crown of the plant; this is achieved by inserting bricks or other inert material under the container to raise it.

There are two main groups of water lilies: the hardy and the tropical. In temperate zones the hardy ones are fine for outdoor ponds; the tropical lilies are only suited to indoor and outdoor ponds where the water temperature is maintained at 21°C (70°F) throughout the year.

The best soil to grow water lilies in

Pygmy water lilies

Pygmy varieties are suitable for small ponds with water to a depth of 23cm (9in). They spread to 1800cm² (2ft²).

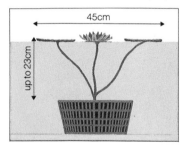

WHITE BLOOMS
candida small cup-shaped flowers with a red stigma.
odorata minor Small and scented blooms of pure white; the green leaves are red underneath.
'Pygmaea Alba' The smallest lily, with flowers barely 2.5cm (1in) across. It requires just 5cm (2in) of water over the crown and needs protection during hard frost.

Right: 'Laydekeri Lilacea', *with fine tiny rose-coloured scented blooms that deepen to red as they mature.*

Far right: 'Comanche' *has pink, orange and yellow blooms that are held well above the water surface.*

PINK AND ROSE BLOOMS
caroliniana Delicate perfumed medium-sized blooms of skin-pink.
'Laydekeri Lilacea' Rose-coloured scented cup-shaped blooms that deepen to red as they age. The leaves are dark green.
odorata 'W.B. Shaw' Very fragrant pink flowers with narrow petals carried above the water surface.

RED BLOOMS
'Ellisiana' Deep red flowers that darken to purple at the centre.
'Laydekeri purpurata' The blooms are bright rosy crimson with shading on the petals. Very free flowering.

is a heavy loam well fortified with bonemeal (approximately 0.1 litres per 4.5 litres of soil). Animal manures are not recommended as the water becomes over rich with nutrients that will encourage algae growth. Should the loam be poor quality and low in nitrogen mix some dried blood into the soil. The roots should be well anchored by ramming the soil well down in the container, leaving some room for a layer of shingle or gravel over the soil to prevent fish from stirring up the fine particles and making the water cloudy.

Water lilies need sun, plain soil and the right depth of water. Given these they will reward the gardener with a prolific show of flowers from early summer onwards.

Above: *Water lilies should be planted in containers filled with a heavy loam with the growing tip just above the surface and a layer of stone chips to stop fish from stirring up the soil.*

'Maurice Laydekeri' Red flowers flecked with white.

pygmaea rubra Delicate rose blooms that age to dark red.

YELLOW AND ORANGE BLOOMS

'Aurora' The blooms start yellow and change to orange and then deepen to red. The leaves are mottled brown and green.

'Comanche' Deep apricot flowers turning to copper with orange centres. Young foliage is purple changing to green mottled with brown. The blooms are held well above the water surface.

'Graziella' Orange blooms. Very free flowering. Blooms 5-7.5cm (2-3in).

'Helvola' The smallest yellow water lily with pale yellow star-shaped flowers and golden centres. Young foliage is purple changing to green mottled with brown. The blooms are held well above the water surface.

'Indiana' Pink-orange blooms that turn to copper-red. Green leaves marked with purple.

odorata sulphureae Small spiky soft yellow flowers held above the water surface. Small spotted leaves.

'Paul Hariot' Yellow flowers that age through orange to red. Free flowering. Leaves marked in brown and green. Blooms 13-15cm (5-6in) across.

Small water lilies

These need 15-45cm (6-18in) of water depth and spread to 60cm (2ft) across when fully mature.

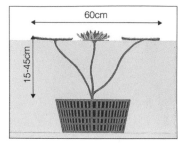

WHITE BLOOMS

'Albatross' Large white flowers with golden centres and erect petals. Young leaves are purple and turn to apple green as they mature.

caroliniana nivea Large prolific blooms for its small size. White and fragrant.

'Hermine' Star-shaped flowers that stand out of the water. Pointed petals; very free flowering.

'Lactae' Delicate pink blooms that fade to white as they age.

'Loose' The flowers are held 30cm (12in) above the water surface. Scented and star-shaped, often 15cm (6in) wide.

PINK AND RED BLOOMS

'Firecrest' Bright pink blooms with orange stamens with red tips.

odorata 'Turicensis' Medium-sized flowers of a soft deep pink. Fragrant with long and rounded petals.

odorata rosea Soft deep pink flowers of medium size, but the plant needs to spread in fairly shallow water and is often treated as a marginal.

'Pink Opal' Scented flowers of a pinky-red; the petals are broad and give a spectacular show.

'Rose Arey' Brilliant rose-pink blooms up to 20cm (8in) across with long pointed petals that are incurved. Free flowering and scented.

'Rose Magnolia' Delicate rose-pink blooms held above the water surface.

'Rose Nymph' Fragrant deep pink flowers that open 18cm (7in) wide.

'Somptuosa' One of the first water lilies to flower. Large semi-double rose-pink blooms that deepen to a deep strawberry pink in the centre.

RED BLOOMS

'Andreana' Large orange-red blooms. Free flowering with green leaves mottled with brown.

'Froebeli' Prolific wine-red flowers. A very reliable variety.

'Gloriosa' Bright red blooms. The growth rate and leaf area of this plant are minimal which, with its prolific flowering, makes it ideal for the smaller pond.

'James Brydon' Prolific bright red blooms. It will stand more shade than most water lilies and has a compact spread that makes it ideal for both

Below: 'Albatross', *a lovely white lily with a yellow centre; its young leaves will mature to bright green.*

small and medium-sized ponds. The leaves are purple to dark green
'Sanguinea' Blood-red flowers and leaves mottled brown on an olive green
'William Falconer' One of the darkest reds, with a yellow centre and a cup-shaped bloom. The foliage is dark green.
'Vesuve' Rich fire-red blooms.

YELLOW AND ORANGE BLOOMS
'Phoebus' Yellow blooms blushed with red and bright orange centres. The foliage is green and purple.

Left: 'Rose Nymph' *has large, beautiful rose-coloured blooms 18cm (7in) wide that are scented.*

Below: 'Gloriosa', *an ideal water lily for the smaller pond. It flowers for a long time with large fragrant blooms.*

'Robinsoniana' Orange-red flowers with lighter yellow-orange centres. The leaves are green heavily marked with purple.
'Sioux' The blooms open a buff-yellow and turn through peach to copper-orange as they age. The foliage is green mottled with brown.
'Solfatare' Star-shaped flowers of a warm yellow. The leaves are green marked with a deep brown-red.

STRIPED BLOOMS
'Darwin' A fragrant lily with red blooms strongly marked with white. The foliage is green.
'Eucharis' Deep pink flowers strikingly spotted and splashed with white.
'Livingstone' Deep cup-shaped scented blooms of red striped with white. Each flower has a deep brown-red centre making a compact shape.

Medium water lilies

These water lilies are suitable for medium-sized ponds. Allow 23-60cm (9-24in) of water over the crowns. The plants have a spread of about 90cm (3ft).

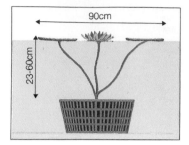

WHITE BLOOMS

'Gonnère' Also known as 'Crystal White' and 'Snowball', this is a semi-double with a profusion of white petals. The leaves are green.

'Hal Miller' Creamy white flowers held above the water surface.

odorata alba White heavily perfumed blooms. The plant prefers shallow water where it can spread.

'Tuberosa' Pure white flowers with golden centres. Apple-green foliage.

marliacea albida Pure white fragrant flowers with yellow centres. The leaves are green with smooth dark brown edges. Vigorous and free

flowering, this is one of the most popular of all water lilies and the most widely planted.

PINK AND ROSE BLOOMS

'Amabilis' Flat star-shaped blooms of rose-pink, darkening as they age. Often up to 23cm (9in) across.

'Brackleyi Rosea' A scented lily of deep pink that fades with age. The free-flowering blooms stand just above the water level. It can occasionally seed itself.

'Fabiola' Rosy red flowers with a deep brown-red centre. The foliage is green.

'Jean de Lamarsalle' Pale pink blooms.

'Mme. Wilfron Gonnère' Double flowers of a rich pink, cup-shaped with the centre flushed rose. The leaves are plain green.

'Mrs. Richmond' Large blooms of deep pink, globe-like in shape with the colour becoming darker towards the centre.

marliacea carnea Also known as 'Morning Glory', this is a very popular plant with large fresh rose-pink blooms. Very free flowering with a vanilla fragrance. A robust plant.

marliacea rosea When this plant first flowers the blooms are barely pink but as it becomes established the colour becomes much stronger and deeper

Above: N. marliacea carnea, *also known as 'Morning Glory', is a very popular and robust water lily that flowers freely with large vanilla-scented fresh rose-pink blooms that are held above the water surface.*

towards the centre. Deeper in colour than marliacea carnea.

'Masaniello' Large flowers of rose deepening towards the centre and becoming darker as the plant matures. Free flowering with peony-shaped blooms.

'Rene Gerard' Red blooms streaked with pink becoming darker towards the centre and with pointed petals. The plant is free flowering but with less prolific leaf growth.

RED BLOOMS

'Attraction' Large flowers up to 25cm (10in) across of a garnet red flecked with white along the edges of the petals. Very free flowering, the young plants have pale pink blooms. Allow plenty of space as it is a vigorous grower.

'Bory de Saint Vincent' Well shaped strong red blooms. The foliage is a plain green.

'Conqueror' Large blooms that are blood red in the centre and have outer petals of a paler red with some white flecking. Often remains open in the evening.

'Escarboucle' A very popular water lily with large flat blooms of rich wine red with pointed petals. Very free flowering and of excellent quality. Well worth growing if you have space.

'Gloriosa' Red-rose blooms that change to deep rose, well scented and a prolific producer of flowers in a long season. Can be grown either in constricted areas or in a large pond.

marliacea rubra punctata Red flowers marked with lilac.

'Newton' Bowl-shaped blooms raised above the surface of the water, orange-red in colour with long gold stamens and pointed petals.

'Rene Gerard' Flowers with slender pointed petals of a rich rose streaked with crimson, becoming deeper towards the centre. Free flowering and with restricted leaf growth.

YELLOW BLOOMS

'Moorei' Pale yellow blooms up to 15cm (6in) wide, well proportioned and full petalled. The foliage is green with brown spots.

odorata sulphurea grandiflora The petals are narrow and plentiful, of a good pale yellow. The blooms are held above the water surface. The leaves are marked and spotted.

'Sunrise' Bright yellow delicately scented flowers with gold stamens held above the water surface. The foliage is dark green with red undersides marked in brown and is borne on hairy stems. Hardy but blooms much better under glass.

Above: 'Mme. Wilfron Gonnère' *has lovely double pink flowers, the petals often speckled with white.*

Above: 'Escarboucle' *has a very attractive bloom of deep red, with pointed petals; it is free flowering.*

Large water lilies

Water lilies for the larger pond that need 23cm-1.2m (9in-4ft) of water above the crown and will spread to over 1.2m (4ft) across.

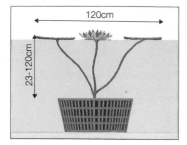

Above: 'Colossea', *a vigorous plant with large fragrant blooms, enjoys deep water and has a long season.*

WHITE BLOOMS

alba A vigorous water lily with white flowers 10-13cm (4-5in) across that is often used in areas of cold, deep and barely moving water where hybrids will not thrive. It quickly becomes established and spreads over a large area.

'Colossea' A plant for larger ponds as it is very vigorous with large scented white blooms. It has a long flowering period and will grow in deep water.

'Gladstoniana' Very large white flowers with golden centres. Needs deep water to expose the 20cm (8in) wide blooms.

tuberosa var. 'Richardsonii' Cup-shaped blooms held just above the water level with several rings of white petals round the centre of gold stamens. Needs deep water and can be vigorous.

'Virginalis' A white water lily with pointed petals regarded by some as the best shaped of all the whites. Free flowering through a long season.

PINK AND ROSE BLOOMS

'Baroness Orczy' Very large deep pink flowers.

'Formosa' Large rose-pink blooms that grow darker as they age, with gold stamens. Free flowering with green foliage.

'Leviathan' Large deep pink scented flowers.

'Mrs. C.W. Thomas' Semi-double pink scented blooms.

tuberosa rosea Scented blooms 10-13cm (4-5in) wide, pink and raised

above the water surface. The foliage is light green and needs plenty of space to grow in width and depth.

RED BLOOMS

'Arethusa' Large globular flowers a deep dark red in the centre fading to deep rose on the outer petals.

atropurpurea Deep crimson to purple blooms about 20cm (8in) across that sit flat on the water surface and open wide to show off the long gold stamens in the centre. Free flowering. The young leaves are purple and mature to dark green.

'Attraction' A free-flowering water lily with deep garnet red blooms up to 25cm (10in) wide, the petals edged with white flecks. Young plants have pale pink blooms that suggest very little of the mature plant's potential. Provide space to show off the beauty of this popular hybrid.

'Charles de Meurville' Large blooms – up to 20cm (8in) wide – of a rich burgundy colour. The leaves are large and the plant needs plenty of space to grow well.

'Picciola' A vigorous lily with large dark crimson blooms about 25cm (10in) across that stand out of the water. The leaves are spotted and marked with dark red on green.

Right: Nymphaea marliacea chromatella, *a well-known yellow lily for the larger pond. It is free flowering.*

YELLOW AND ORANGE BLOOMS
'Colonel A.J. Welch' A water lily that is only recommended for deep water, which it stands better than marliacea chromatella. The yellow flowers are outweighed by the prolific leaves. The blooms stand well above the water surface. Faintly marbled foliage.
marliacea chromatella Large primrose yellow flowers 15-18cm (6-7in) across, full petalled and with

Above: *'Formosa' has large rose-pink free-flowering blooms that darken with age and attractive gold stamens.*

good proportions. Reliably free flowering over a long season. The large green leaves are blotched with dark brown. The plant has been in cultivation for over a hundred years and is still very popular for the larger pond. A lovely water lily.

Bog plants

Stretches of open water are often surrounded by wetlands, areas of constantly moist soil where the water table is just beneath the surface. A number of plants have adapted their root system to cope with this high moisture level. Many of these 'bog plants' have brightly coloured flowers and interesting leaf shapes and make fine subjects for planting near a garden pond. Try growing some from the following selection.

Aconitum (1)
Monkshood; Wolf's Bane
Of this large family of plants, two are recommended: *A. carmichaelii* from Central China, 1.8m (6ft) tall with dark green foliage and blue flowers, and *A. napellus* from Europe and Asia, up to 1.2m (4ft) high with deeply cut leaves and violet-blue flowers. Increase by root division or by seed. Beware: all parts of the plant are poisonous.

Astilbe (2)
False Goat's Beard
A large group of plants from Europe and Asia. The most suitable ones are the *A. arendsii* hybrids, which bear white, pink, red and crimson blooms. The foliage is mid to deep green and deeply divided. The superb flowerheads are feathery and made up of tiny flowers. They appear throughout the summer months. Most of these plants will grow 60-90cm (2-3ft) high. Propagate astilbes by dividing the clumps in spring.

Camassia (3)
Quamash
A North American bulbous plant with sword-like leaves and spikes of purple, blue, white and cream flowers in early summer. A double variety is available. The plant grows to 90cm (3ft) tall and can be increased by division of the bulbs or by seed.

1   2   3   4

Claytonia (4)
Arctic Spring Beauty
A group of small plants from North America and Asia with fleshy rootstocks, smooth leaves and white or pink flowers in spring. *C. arctica*, *C. sibirica* and *C. virginica* all grow up to 15cm (6in) tall and thrive in peaty bog conditions. Increase by seed.

Eupatorium (5)
Hemp Agrimony
A large family from the Northern Hemisphere comprising shrubby and herbaceous plants with varying leaves and large heads of daisy-like flowers in white, pink and purple from midsummer until early autumn. Usually growing up to 1.2m (4ft) tall some, such as *E. cannabinum*, can reach 1.8m (6ft) in a rich and moist soil. Cut the stems almost to ground level after flowering and increase by dividing the rootstock.

Filipendulina (6)
Dropwort
From Europe, Asia and North America, these plants are like *Spiraea*, to which they are closely related. They have long green leaves in a variety of shapes, mainly lobed, and large heads of small white, pink or red flowers. Some varieties can reach 2.4m (8ft) tall, but most grow to 90cm (3ft). Increase by root division.

Gunnera manicata (7)
A striking Brazilian plant that looks like a giant rhubarb. The leaves can reach 3m (10ft) long by 2.4m (8ft) wide and the flowers are like long circular brushes 1m (3.3ft) tall. Frost will cut the foliage back, but if the crown is covered with a layer of leaves or bracken it will survive the winter. The plant can reach 4.5m (15ft) high and 6m (20ft) wide, making it suitable only for the larger garden. Divide plants.

5   6   7

Helonius bullata
Swamp Pink; Stud Flower
A North American plant with shiny leaves clustered in rosettes and spikes of pink flowers in spring. It grows up to 45cm (18in) tall and has a tuberous rooted system that can be divided for increasing stock.

Heloniopsis
Two Japanese spring-flowering plants, *H. breviscarpa* with white flowers and *H. japonica* with pink blooms, are recommended. Both have spear-shaped leaves and should reach 30cm (12in) tall in a good moist soil. *H. breviscarpa* sometimes increases by producing small plants on its leaf ends; otherwise divide the rootstock.

Hemerocallis (1)
Day Lily
The best of this group of plants come from China. They have sword-like leaves and many hybrids are available to provide a wide range of midsummer colour. They will reach 60-107cm (2-3.5ft) tall and can be increased by root division in spring.

Hosta (3)
Funkia
Most hostas originate in Japan and are grown for their fine decorative foliage and their ability to thrive in shade. The leaves are veined and are available in blue, yellow, green and variegations. The flower spikes, white or mauve in colour, appear in early summer. Plants grow to 75cm (30in) in height. Increase by division in the spring. Guard against slug damage.

Iris (4)
A large group of plants containing some species that thrive in moist conditions. Most come from China and have sword-like leaves and fine iris blooms, some heavily marked and

1   2   3   4

veined. Recommended are: *Iris bulleyana*, *I. chrysographes*, *I. forestii*, *I. kaempferi*, *I. laevigata*, *I. sibirica* and *I. wilsonii*. *I. kaempferi* needs to be kept dry during the winter months. Normally increased by division. (See also description of irises under 'Deep water and marginal plants' page 58.)

Ligularia (5)
Mainly of Chinese and Japanese origin, most ligularias have heart-shaped leaves and spikes of yellow and orange daisy-like flowers in summer. They can thrive in a deep moist soil and can reach 1.5m (5ft) tall. Increase by division in spring.

Lobelia (2)
A few of the American members of this family will thrive by the pond: *L. cardinalis*, with oblong leaves and spikes of red flowers; *L. fulgens* and its hybrids, with purple and red foliage; and *L. syphilitica*, with blue or white flowers. All grow up to 90cm (3ft) tall and can be increased by root division during the spring.

Lysichitum (6)
Two spring-flowering plants, *L. americanum* from America, with large yellow flowers and pointed green leaves, and *L. camschatense* from Japan, with white flowers like the Arum Lily can be recommended. They are easily grown in either shallow water or wet soil, in sun or partial shade. Up to 90cm (3ft) tall and easily raised from seed.

Primulas (7)
Most of the moisture-loving primulas come from Eastern Asia and have a variety of forms; the flowers can be single or in umbels of up to 50 blooms in a variety of colours. Some will reach up to 90cm (3ft) tall while others will only make 15cm (16in) in height. They can be grown from seed or division.

5   6   7

Fishes for garden ponds

One of the most exciting aspects of the garden pond is the livestock that it can support. Of these, the most spectacular and interesting are the fishes, which provide a continuous movement and sparkle that people of all ages find fascinating. The golden varieties of fish are the most easily seen and appreciated; the dark green varieties are well camouflaged and need patience to see them and watch their movements. The brighter fish are more vulnerable to predators, and a sufficient cover of plant life in the pond is necessary for their protection.

Fishes are important to the pond environment, as they take in oxygen from the water and then expel carbon dioxide through their gills; the carbon dioxide is then absorbed into the plant tissues along with water. Carbon, hydrogen and oxygen are processed within the plant with the sun's rays, a process called photosynthesis, giving off surplus oxygen into the water for the fishes to

take up again and repeat the cycle for the benefit of both fishes and plants. At night the process is reversed, with the plants taking up oxygen and releasing carbon dioxide. This can cause a low level of oxygen in the morning making the fishes sluggish. As soon as the sun rays start working on the plant life the oxygen starts moving again.

Some fishes are scavengers, acting as unwitting cleaners in the pond by taking up debris from the pond floor and water as food. It is advisable to cover all soil with a layer of stones or gravel to prevent the soil being stirred up and clouding the water, stopping the fishes from being seen clearly in the pond.

If you intend to keep fishes in your pool, then it will be particularly important to ensure that water quality is good (see pages 16-17). You should consider installing a biological filter to remove waste created by the fish.

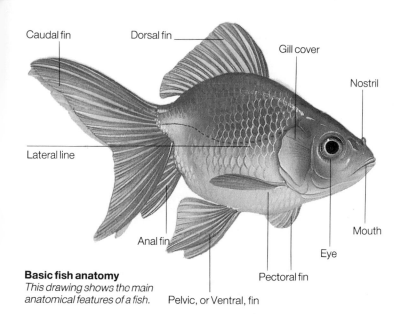

Caudal fin

Dorsal fin

Gill cover

Nostril

Lateral line

Anal fin

Mouth

Eye

Basic fish anatomy
*This drawing shows the main
anatomical features of a fish.*

Pelvic, or Ventral, fin

Pectoral fin

Common Goldfish

(*Carassius auratus*)
Some authorities claim that it was due
to the high mineral content of the
water in some volcanic areas of China
and Japan that the black pigment in
some fishes was lost, leaving only a
gold colour. From these fishes there
have been developed many fancy
breeds; over 120 different varieties
are recorded, but the Common
Goldfish is still the most popular and
the cheapest of this group. It has a
bright red-gold metallic appearance,
is scaled, and should have a broad
short head with a small mouth, bright
eyes, and the back and belly gently
arched. The dorsal fin starts on the
peak of the back, and the stiff caudal
fin is moderately forked; the rest of the
fins are held stiffly.

There are other colours available.
Yellow-gold varieties are known as
Canaries, white ones are called
Pearls, and spotted or blotched ones
are referred to as Orioles. Goldfishes
will grow to over 13cm (5in) long.

Left: *The Common Goldfish is the
hardiest and most popular of pond
fish with its bright metallic colour.*

Shubunkin

These are sometimes called Harlequin or Speckled Goldfishes, and are developed from the Common Goldfish. The Shubunkin has transparent scales that are not shiny, as the fish lacks reflective tissue and has no metallic gleam, so it appears scaleless. This skin condition allows the deeper layers to show through giving a mottled mixture of yellow, red, brown, bright blue, violet, black and white; it is also available in plain colours. The colours should spread into the fins. Some fishes have a greater proportion of blue in their make-up than the normal Shubunkin and are classified as Blue Shubunkins. Shubunkins that resemble the Common Goldfish in shape are known as London Shubunkins; those with a much larger caudal fin with rounded lobes are known as Bristol Shubunkins.

These fishes are hardy and can be left out in the pond to overwinter. They are larger than the Common Goldfish and much faster in their movements, and they should be allowed plenty of space to swim and manoeuvre in the pond. The Shubunkin will become quite tame and may take food from the hand.

Fantail

This fish is also known as the Fringetail, and is more rounded with a deeper body than the Shubunkin or the Common Goldfish, giving it an egg-shaped appearance. It should have no hump to the back, but form a good curve. The height of the dorsal fin should be about half the body depth and held stiffly; the caudal fin has well-forked twin fins, so that viewed from behind it looks like an inverted Y. The colour is red-gold and the body shiny or with a pearly sheen.

It is not too hardy and during the winter months it should be lifted from the pond and moved indoors to a frost-free situation where the water can be kept at a temperature of 10-16°C (50-60°F). These attractive fish are noted for their long flowing tails and large rounded bodies.

Below: *A Bristol-type Shubunkin; its large caudal fin has rounded lobes. The fish's skin appears scaleless.*

Above: *Fantails with egg-shaped bodies and fine colour. They would grace any pool; keep frost-free.*

Below: *A Blue Shubunkin. These are highly prized for varied colour patterns and will become quite tame in time.*

79

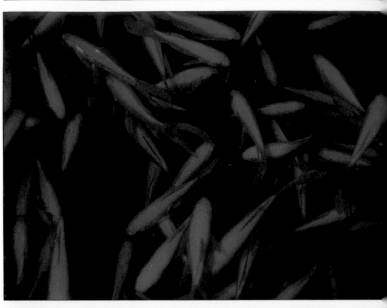

Comet

Also known as a Longtail, this is one of the fastest and most graceful of the Goldfish varieties. It is similar to the Shubunkin, but the longer caudal fin is deeply forked and at least three-quarters the length of the body. The other fins are flowing but very functional, making the fish very agile. The tail fin is single. The Comet is generally red, and shinier than the Shubunkin, but some are yellow; the preferred colour is a deep red-orange. Blue varieties are called Blue

Left: *A shoal of Comets. These are very fast and agile in the water, providing a continuous spectacle.*

Above: *The Sarasa Comets are noted for their bright red markings on a white background; they are hardy.*

Comets, and Sarasa Comets have strong red markings on a white background.

Comets are quite hardy and can be left to overwinter in the pond, although a pond heater is beneficial, and keeps the surface partly clear of

Above: *Comets are available in many colours, and the blue varieties are highly prized because of their rarity.*

ice. This fish is highly recommended for the garden pond, because of its brilliant colour and movement.

Veiltail

This Goldfish variety is sometimes also known as a Fringetail. It is noted for its body depth, which is more than half the body length, and the dorsal fin is three-quarters the body depth, which makes the fish egg-shaped. The drooping caudal fin is long and broad, with square-cut lower edges, and it forms graceful folds like fine lace. The tail can be double, triple, or even quadruple. The rest of the fins are long and paired; they are vulnerable and liable to be damaged by other fishes or by sharp projections in the pond. The eyes can be normal, or may project. There is much variety in the fish's colour; this can be either scaled or metallic-looking, or transparent with the appearance of mother-of-pearl.

The Veiltail is slow in the pond, and is best kept in a separate pond, as faster fish usually reach the food first to the detriment of the slower swimmer. Protect this variety during winter by keeping it in an indoor pond.

Below: *The Veiltail has a body of disproportionate depth, with a long, broad and drooping caudal fin that looks like very fine lace.*

Telescope

This variety of the Common Goldfish is sometimes called the Pop-eyed Goldfish or Dragon Eyes. It can have either a metallic scaled skin or an opalescent transparent one. It has a short deep body, with in many cases a hump on the back at the junction with the head along the dorsal curve. Its curious eyes protrude almost on stalks. The fish is normally a bright orange and white but it can also be obtained in blue and black. The fins are large and often out of proportion with the body; the caudal fin is much

Above: *The Telescope, a rather lumpy and tender Goldfish, has curious eyes that project out from the head; it needs to be protected from frost.*

longer than the trunk and very delicate, which makes it vulnerable to damage from other fishes and from rough stones.

As this variety is less hardy than other Common Goldfishes it is best removed from the pond in autumn, kept indoors in a water temperature of 10-16°C (50-60°F), then returned to the pond during the spring.

Above: *A Moor, with its velvety black colouring that is only conspicuous in a pond made from pale materials, is accordingly not a common pond fish.*

Right: *The Oranda has a warty growth on the head like a hood, which should be symmetrical. Prone to disease, the fish also needs to be kept frost-free.*

Below: *A Red Cap Oranda has a red warty hood that forms a distinctive feature on the white or silver body.*

Moor

Often called the Black Moor, this fish has much the appearance of a Veiltail in the shape of its body and the arrangement of the fins and drooping tail, and the eyes protrude like those of a Telescope; but the colouring is velvety black, which turns to dark brown as the fish ages. This colouring makes it a poor fish for the garden pond, as it is not easily seen unless the pond is constructed from a pale-coloured material. They are also more susceptible to disease and damage than the ordinary Common Goldfish.

The Moor is not hardy, and should be lifted out of the pond in autumn and kept through the winter indoors in water that should not drop below 13°C (55°F) to keep the fish active. It is a slow swimmer and needs to be kept with other slow fish only, so that they can feed at their own pace and not have their food removed and eaten by faster fishes in the pond.

Oranda

This Goldfish has a warty growth that covers most of the head. The fish is red, and not unlike the Veiltail in shape, with a broad short head. The 'hood' should be symmetrical, and leave only the mouth and eyes exposed. These grotesque fishes are more likely to suffer from disease than the Common Goldfish.

They are not hardy and should be lifted from the pond in autumn and brought into a frost-free situation for the winter; this will prolong their life.

They need water at a temperature of 13°C (55°F) in winter. The Oranda should be kept with other slow-swimming fishes.

Lionhead

This fish has extraordinary wart-like growths on its head which look out of proportion to the rest of it. These growths should be symmetrical for it to be of value. The Lionhead is like an Oranda but has no dorsal fin; the caudal fin is small and rounded, and the pelvic, anal and pectoral fins are rounded. The fish can either be scaled and metallic-looking or it can have transparent scales that give an opalescent effect. Usually it is red. Watch for poor health.

In winter keep the Lionhead in an indoor aquarium protected from frost; the water should be 13°C (55°F) for it to be active. The Lionhead is a slow swimmer and should be kept with other slow fish so that they have equal opportunities to find and eat food.

Celestial

This fish, also known as the Skygazer, has telescopic-like eyes that turn upwards. Some varieties are scaled and look metallic, whereas others have a pearly sheen. The body is long,

and there is no dorsal fin. The Celestial should be kept on its own, and not mixed with other fishes, as it is at a disadvantage when competing for food because it looks in the wrong direction all the time.

It is not hardy, and in winter should be transferred from the outdoor pond to a frost-free situation where the water can be kept at a temperature of 13°C (55°F); in spring, when the danger of frost has passed, it can be returned to the pond. As it is a slow swimmer it needs to be watched for signs of disease or distress; it has the reputation of being short-lived.

Below: *A Lionhead has an encrusted head, covered with wart-like growths which should be symmetrical in shape. The fish is quite like an Oranda but has no dorsal fin.*

Inset below: *The Celestial is not unlike a Telescope but looks up skywards; it is a very slow swimmer and because of its constant upward gaze has trouble finding food.*

87

Nishikigoi – Fancy Koi

Koi are carp (*Cyprinus carpio*) and were first mentioned in Japan some 1600 years ago, when coloured varieties were kept for decoration in ponds. Over the years these fishes have been more fully developed by careful breeding and selection, to give us today a wide variety of forms and colours. They are particularly popular for garden pools because of their large size, brilliant colours, long life, character and stamina.

They can be seen easily because of their size and vivid colours. They also grow quickly, and may become sufficiently tame to eat out of your hand. Koi can be left in the pond through the winter, provided the water remains just above freezing point. As they are bottom-feeders, they will stir up any soil that is exposed, clouding the water; it is therefore important to cover all the soil with gravel or stone chips.

Koi can grow to some 90cm (36in) long and need plenty of water to swim in, with a minimum depth of 1.5m (5ft) to give the fishes a frost-free area in winter. If you live where temperatures are likely to be consistently below zero, a cover for the pond and a heater are advisable. When calculating the number of fishes, allow at least 2.5m^2 (27ft^2) for each Koi, to allow for growth and for sufficient food to be produced for it. Some water movement is important to keep the oxygen level high, particularly in the early morning and in hot stormy weather.

Although Koi can be sub-divided into the two groups of Japanese and German Koi (the former slimmer than the latter), the main classification is by colour and pattern.. The colour is derived from the basic pigments in the fish and can be black, white, yellow, blue or red.

Below: *The large size of the fancy Koi and their spectacular colouring give movement to a garden pool.*

Top: *A pair of colourful Koi that would provide interest in any stretch of water for a long time, although they do need plenty of room for good health.*

Above: *The brilliant colouring and unusual markings of these long living Koi make them very popular, especially when they become tame.*

Shiro Muji is a white Koi, pure and unmarked.

Aka Muji is red.

Karasu Goi is a black Koi, but some have white markings.

Asagi has a back covered with blue scales with a lighter blue between, giving it a netted look.

Kohaku (Red-white) is basically a pure white fish with deep red markings, the edges of which should be sharp and clean; the markings preferably start with a red spot on the head and finish with a red spot on the trunk before the caudal fin. There are various sub-groups, defined by the nature and balance of the markings.

Taisho Sanke (Japanese Tricolour) is a pure white Koi with red and black patterns; there should be a large red spot on the head, and the patterns must be clear and distinct.

Showa Sanke (Modern Japanese Tricolour) is a black Koi with red and white markings. The main difference between this and the previous group

Below: *Showa Sanke, a black Koi with red and white markings.*

Below: *Taisho Sanke is a pure white Koi with red and black patterns.*

Below: *Tancho Kohaku is a Koi with a white body and red spot on the head.*

Below: *Kikusui has a white base with orange wave patterns over it.*

is that the main colour has to wrap right round the trunk of the fish. Again there are sub-groups within this section, depending on the type, size and colouring of the patterns.

Ohgon (Gold) is a pale overall gold.

Yamabuki Ohgon (Yellow Rose Ohgon) is a cross between a yellow Koi and an Ohgon, it is a spectacular fish with metallic scales.

Hariwake Ohgon is a patterned fish with clearly divided patterns of gold and silver, and of a metallic sheen.

Shiro Utsuri is a black Koi with white markings that make a bold and distinct pattern.

Ki Utsuri and Hi Utsuri: the former looks like the Shiro Utsuri but with yellow markings instead of white ones, and the Hi Utsuri has red markings on the black base.

Kinsui and Ginsui are metallic-looking fishes with either gold (Kinsui) or silver (Ginsui) overall colour. These Koi are spectacular but the brilliance fades after a year or two.

Below: *Ohgon is a Koi with a light gold body and clear metallic scales.*

Below: *Hariwake Ohgon has a silver base with golden patterns over it.*

Below: *A collection of Koi shows the brilliant variety of colours available,* from the pure silver-white through the two-coloured to the tri-coloured ones.

91

Other coldwater fishes

Golden Orfe
(Idus idus)
This fish is lively and provides a lot of interest in the pond. If kept as a single fish or in a single pair it is shy and rarely seen, but in a shoal it is much more confident, moving quickly and darting out in the open areas of water, and rising to take food from the surface. It is a small hardy fish with a pale golden colour that fades to silver as it nears the dorsal curve, the fins retaining a stronger colour; a silver variety is also available.

The Golden Orfe is long and slender, reaching 30cm (12in) in length. It is an excellent scavenger, removing insects and mosquito larvae from plants and from the water surface. It is best kept in a spacious pond where it can have a good length to swim in; it has been known to jump right out of small ponds. During the winter months it is less active and keeps away from the surface, preferring to lie dormant near the pond bottom.

Above: *Golden Orfe, a very popular fish that is fast and spectacular when kept in a shoal, but shy when kept as a pair or a single fish.*

Golden Rudd
(*Scardinius erythrophthalmus*)
This very attractive fish has a silvery colour with a golden hue. The scales are large, rough and distinct. The eyes and fins are red, and the pectoral, pelvic and anal fins are darker than the dorsal fin. It is often confused with the Roach (*Rutilus rutilus*), but is distinguishable because its dorsal fin starts well back on the spine, between the anal and pelvic fins.

The Golden Rudd will grow to 45cm (18in) in length, and may reach 2kg (4lb 6oz) in weight. It feeds on worms and ant eggs as well as aquatic vegetation. It is found wild in slow-running rivers and lakes in most parts of Europe. The Golden Rudd lays eggs among weeds, and they

Left: *Golden Rudd can grow to quite a large size for a garden pond; 45cm (18in) long and 2kg (4lb 6oz) in weight. It is hardy and attractive.*

hatch in five to eight days. It is quite like the Golden Orfe, of a better shape but not so bright in colour. This hardy species thrives in the open pond, where it lives well with other fishes.

Green Tench
(*Tinca tinca*)
This very hardy fish will live a long time out of water. It grows well and increases quickly in still water, which it prefers to running water. The skin is slimy and this is reputed to cure various diseases on other fishes in the pond. Its natural food consists of insects, worms and young shoots of water vegetation. It will increase quickly where the conditions are right, and two males should be provided for each female; the sexes can be distinguished by the size of the pelvic fin, which is larger in the male. The mouth has a barbel on each side.

This fish is dark green in colour, with pink lips and very dark green fins. When mature it may reach a length of 45cm (18in), and weigh up to 2.5kg (5lb 8oz). These fishes are excellent scavengers as they always eat off the bottom of the pond. They are often found in rivers, ponds and sand pits.

Golden Tench
(*Tinca tinca*)
The Golden Tench, a variety of the Green Tench, is an excellent fish to add to the pond. It is golden with a yellow hue. The mouth is toothless with a small barbel at each side, blunt and leathery. The fine scales are covered with a mucus that gives it a slimy feel. The dorsal and anal fins are without bony rays, and the shape of the caudal fin varies with the age of the fish: concave when young, straight as it matures and convex when old.

This variety will increase rapidly if two males (which have larger pelvic fins than the female) are provided to each female. The Golden Tench enjoys insects and worms, and is a scavenger that invariably eats off the pond bottom. When the fish is fully grown it can reach almost 45cm (18in) and up to 2.5kg (5lb 8oz).

Below: *A shoal of young Minnows that provide a flash of movement to a pond, growing to a finger's length.*

Minnow
(*Phoxinus phoxinus*)
These small fishes are found in the wild in many streams, ponds and rivers, and they readily settle into pond life. They prefer to live in shoals, where they are very active and give plenty of movement to the water. They live for quite a long time, and individuals have been known to survive for 12 years in a pond. In spring the male minnow changes colour from its original olive-brown to a green flushed with red. The female will spawn on gravel, and the eggs hatch in about ten days.

With a change in the surroundings Minnows will change colour, turning lighter or darker according to the background. The dorsal fin is placed well back, over the space between the pectoral and anal fins. The tail is forked, with large spots at the base. The fish has a total length of some 7.5cm (3in). Minnows are hardy, and bold in taking food from larger fishes; they enjoy flies, meat and worms.

Above: *The Common Trout are a great challenge to fishkeepers: they need an especially high oxygen level.*

Below: *Mirror Carp are not as showy as some fish but they can be farmed for food and can be kept as pets.*

For that extra challenge

There are a number of other fish that can be kept in a coldwater pond, but are less decorative or require more specialized treatment than the Common Goldfish. These are probably best reserved for the more enthusiastic fishkeeper when the more common fishes start to become less interesting.

The various Carps such as the Crucian Carp (*Carassius carassius*), the Leather and Mirror Carps (*Cyprinus carpio*), and the Prussian Carp (*Carassius auratus gibelio*) are likely to be less noticeable in the outdoor pond, but some of these are suitable for food-farming. The most

popular of the food fishes are the Trouts, either the Rainbow Trout (*Salmo gairdneri*) or the Common Trout (*Salmo trutta*) but they do need a higher oxygen level in the water. This can be achieved by using a more powerful pump to move a larger quantity of water. Also, as the oxygen requirements are so high, less Trout can be accommodated in the pond compared with other species.

Some 'tropical' freshwater fishes can be kept successfully in outdoor ponds – at least during the summer months in temperate climates. These include Japanese Ricefish (*Oryzias latipes*) and White Cloud Mountain Minnow (*Tanichthys albonubes*).

95

Other pond livestock

Apart from the livestock deliberately introduced into the water, other forms creep in uninvited, but most of these are beneficial, either keeping the pond clean or providing a ready meal for the fishes. Others are more trouble, however, causing damage to fish and plant life, especially the small fry and the young fresh growth; it is important to keep an eye on the health of the pond life and spot any damage to fishes or plants that may have been caused by an unwanted guest. Among the vast amount of livestock it is quite difficult to determine which is friend and which is foe, and it is impossible to keep an outdoor pond free from the visitations of insects and other life forms.

Snails

One of the few animals that needs to be introduced into the pond is the snail. There are a number of aquatic snails that will happily feed on debris and help to keep the pond clean without feeding on the plant life.

Planorbis corneus (the Ramshorn Snail) can be put into the pool to clean up unwanted rubbish. It is easily recognized by its handsome flat coiled shell, and breeds well. It will not damage useful vegetation, and is readily available from aquatic dealers.

Viviparus viviparus (the Freshwater Winkle) delights in feeding on dead and decaying vegetation, and is popular with fishkeepers. If disturbed it will cling very tightly to whatever it is attached to, resisting any attempt to pull it off, no matter how hard.

Viviparus fasciatus is very similar to *V. viviparus*, and also eats decaying plant life; but it is also completely different, in that it releases itself the moment it is touched.

Most of the other snails that are found in the pond introduce themselves and can be left to populate the water unless they are seen to feed on your prize aquatics. Some are small and insignificant, others are larger. Some of the bigger snails are from the

Below: *The Common Frog,* Rana temporaria, *is a welcome visitor to the pool, often consuming unwanted pests such as slugs and snails.*

Lymnaea family, which includes the Great Pond Snail (*Lymnaea stagnalis*), a snail that through indiscriminate feeding can cause a lot of damage and should be removed.

Amphibians

Amphibians visit the pond to lay their eggs or spawn; some fishkeepers find

Below: *The Common Toad,* Bufo bufo, *will lay spawn in the spring, but any disadvantage is outweighed by the insects that they consume.*

Above: *Common or Smooth Newt,* Triturus vulgaris, *comes to the pond to breed in spring and summer.*

the spawn unsightly and remove it, but the young are beneficial to the balance of life in the water. Young tadpoles are excellent scavengers, starting off by eating vegetable matter and progressing to animal foods. Frogs, toads and newts should all be welcome because they do so much good in the garden, removing unwanted pests such as insects.

Above: *A Dragonfly performs very swift and agile movements in flight which, coupled with its brilliant colouring, gives any pool interest.*

Below: *There are many varieties of Caddis Fly, most of which have interesting larvae that form homes of fine particles of stone or shell.*

Beetles and other insects

There are well over 200 different species of aquatic beetle; some of these are savage and carnivorous, attacking fish and other water animals, but most are happy scavenging among the debris and keeping the pond clean. Unless attacks are seen, it is best to leave most beetles alone.

Surface walkers are often seen traversing the water relying on the surface tension to stop themselves sinking. The best-known of these is *Gerris najas* (the Pond Skater), which literally walks across the water on the lookout for dead or dying insects.

There are a large number of flies that leave their eggs in or close to water, from the humble midges and gnats to the larger caddis flies and dragonflies. Their eggs turn into larvae that prey on lower water creatures, other larvae and tiny fishes, and they in turn become food for larger fishes. There are over 160 different kinds of caddis fly. One of the commonest is *Phryganea grandis* with pale grey-brown wings and yellow-ringed antennae; it folds its wings along its body when at rest, like all the caddis flies. Their larvae form cases or tubes from fine particles of vegetation, stones, sand or shell to live in until the next stage in their development into flying insects.

The dragonflies form a large group of insects well-known for their spectacular colouring and erratic flight pattern. Their eggs are laid on the water surface and then sink to the bottom. When the larvae are hatched they form burrows in which they lie low, preying on small aquatic animal life; then they gradually change until they eventually become flying insects. Dragonfly larvae (nymphs) can be considered a pest and are further described on page 104. Among the other flies are *Culex pipiens* (the Common Gnat) and *Chaoborus* sp. (the Midge). The larvae of these are a good food for fishes, and anyone who fails to keep fishes in the garden pond is likely to become aware of a subsequent noticeable increase in the gnat and midge population.

Other freshwater creatures
Among the other forms of water life is *Argyroneta aquatica* (the Water Spider), which manages to live and nest under water without drowning, due to the air secreted between the hairs on its body; it feeds on land and aquatic animals. Aquatic worms such as *Tubifex* are very similar to the common earthworm, but of a transparent red colour; they provide a useful source of food for the rest of the pond's carnivorous animals. Among the crustaceans that live in fresh water is *Gammarus* sp. (the Freshwater Shrimp), which is a good scavenger and provides food for fishes, particularly trout. *Asellus* sp. (the Water Louse) is another scavenger, and lives on decaying vegetable matter.

Above: *The Red-eyed Damselfly is a lesser form of Dragonfly that provides interest around the pool with its colouring and erratic flight pattern. It lays eggs in the water, many of which then become food for fish.*

Pool upkeep

One is often asked about the amount of upkeep or maintenance a pond requires, but the answer depends on a number of factors that vary from pond to pond. One pond may need very little care, whereas another, due to its size, the plants and fishes that it has been stocked with, and the type of water and construction used, will need a steady flow of attention throughout the year.

Let us take as an example a pond that has a complicated shape with narrow inlets, shallow shelving water and overhanging trees. The shape will at once encourage parts of the water to stagnate; the shallows will breed algae; and leaves will drop from the trees into the water, causing putrefaction. The insect population will increase in certain groups, weeds will run riot, and diseases affecting plants and fishes will increase too.

If we take an alternative pond, with a simple shape so that the water can circulate freely, placed in the open with a balance of plants and livestock, then the amount of attention it needs will be minimal – only an occasional thinning of plants if they become too rampant, and checking the fishes for health and vigour.

Leaves

If you live in a wooded area, autumn leaves can be a problem, falling into the water and sinking to the bottom where they decompose and give off noxious gases. To prevent this occurring, spread a fine net over the water surface to catch the leaves; where there is a large stretch of water, lay the net in sections across the pond so that they can be lifted off piecemeal to remove the leaves.

Weather problems

Weather, too, can cause some additional upkeep. Frost may seal off the water surface, preventing oxygen from reaching the unfrozen water and stopping toxic gases escaping; this is not critical over a short period, as the cold will have made the fishes slow down and they need less oxygen, but there is a danger of ice expanding and cracking or splitting the pond container, whether it is a precast shell, a liner or a concrete pond.

If the pond has been designed with sloping sides the ice will be forced upwards without damaging the structure. A pond heater can be floated in the pond; when switched on, this will keep a small area unfrozen around it, allowing both oxygen and fishes to reach the surface, and when the ice expands the pond container will not be damaged. A cheaper method is to drop a large floating ball into the water, and remove it when the water freezes, to leave a hole in the ice for air

Tall canes will obstruct a heron's flight path and deter it from robbing the pool of pet fish.

Nets are important to lift fish for health examination, as is the spiky tool for removing pondweed.

To prevent ice from sealing the water surface, a pond heater is highly recommended.

to reach the unfrozen water; replace it at night when the temperature drops. The expanding ice will lift the ball, and thus also lower the risk of pond damage by relieving pressure.

Never break the ice with a heavy blow, because the shock waves will pass through the water and can stun or kill the fishes. It is better to use a hot object, a metal bar or a can filled with boiling water, to melt the ice, which can then be lifted off and broken up away from the pond. Sometimes if the weather continues freezing it pays to drain off some water under the ice, leaving 2.5cm (1in) or so of air between ice and water; this will act as a form of insulation, and still keep some oxygen in touch with the water.

In very hot weather there is a danger that a small pond will get too warm and the oxygen level become dangerously low, causing the death of the fishes. To prevent this, increase the level of oxygen by pumping the water through a fountain; the drops of water will be recharged with oxygen before returning to the pond.

Drainpipes should be laid in the pool in winter to give some protection to the fish from predators.

A net stretched over the pool will deter birds and cats and stop dead leaves from dropping in the pond.

Plants can be lifted out for division or examination for pests and aquatic diseases.

At the end of the season the pump has to be lifted out and serviced and thoroughly cleaned.

The health and safety of the pool can be kept at a high level by a little care and regular maintenance to prevent trouble before it starts.

Plants can be gently lowered into the pond, resting on bricks for the soil to absorb water.

Extra oxygenating plants are helpful in hot weather to increase the oxygen level in the water.

When removing fish from the pool while repair or cleaning is undertaking, keep them in a suitable stock pond or, failing that, in a wide-necked vessel (not a jam jar) so that the maximum amount of air can reach the surface.

If the water is acid, a piece of limestone or chalk can be put in it to balance it.

In hot weather when the oxygen level is low, keep the pump running to aerate the water.

Additional oxygenating plants will absorb the carbon dioxide given out by the fishes and return oxygen to the water, and help the pond balance; they will also prevent sunlight from reaching some areas of water and thus stop the growth and spread of algae, which increase in hot weather.

Another thing to watch for in hot weather is the rapid evaporation of water. This can lower the surface quite dramaticaly and expose the liner, if one has been used; sunlight on exposed plastic can speed up deterioration, making the liner brittle and hard so that it cracks, allowing the water to seep away.

When the pond level drops, top it up using a hose. Because the water needs time to adjust to the surrounding temperature, it is better to top up with a little extra water several times, rather than to allow the surface to drop a long way and then have to pour in large quantities

of raw tap water. A little tap water will dilute with the pond water, and the chlorine and other minerals will have time to disperse before the next topping up takes place; this will cause less distress to the livestock.

Occasionally the pond will have a sudden influx of algae, usually after aquatic plants have been thinned out and fed, especially if this coincides with a period of uninterrupted sunshine. This sometimes happens when you wish to show off the pond to friends, and an immediate remedy is called for. The answer is to use a dose of algaecide, which can be obtained from most aquatic centres and specialist shops.

If the water becomes too acid, due to rain or seepage, it is important to redress the balance. This can be done by placing a lump of limestone or chalk in the water until it becomes neutral again. Use a water testing kit to check the pH value finally.

Watch during the summer to keep the pool in good condition and healthy.

Watch for fish hidden in dense growth when lifting out plants for yearly examination.

Should hot weather evaporate too much water, trickle in fresh to make up loss.

Check for leaks and use a repair kit to make good; otherwise it may be necessary to drain the pond to make repairs.

Structural repairs

Leaks can occur with most ponds, but are more likely to happen if you use cheaper materials than with the more expensive and robust ones. The commonest problem is the accidental piercing of the liner with a sharp point, which permits the water to seep away. Kits are supplied by the manufacturers for repairing this type of damage, and the manufacturer's instructions should be followed to ensure a good and lasting repair. This also goes for the precast pool shells.

With concrete the process is more difficult, and often entails draining, cleaning and painting the entire pond area with a repair medium, which can be either a liquid plastic or a bitumen-based paint. An alternative that has become quite popular is to line the concrete pond with a liner.

On the rare occasions when the pond has to be drained – either for repair or to remove debris, overgrown plants or too many fishes – a temporary pond should be set up. This can be made by using a piece of liner material laid inside a large box; or use a series of large bottles with wide mouths or large plastic containers, if they have a large water surface open to the air. The fishes should be caught with a net and transferred into a smooth plastic bowl before taking them out of the pond; this will prevent damage to their scales and the subsequent danger of disease.

Plants can be lifted out, but check that there are no fishes secreted in the matt of stems and leaves. Remove the remaining livestock by hand. Clean or repair the pond and refill it with water. Allow the chlorine to disperse before replacing the plants, and then gradually put back the cheapest fishes first to test the water; if they are fine, then add your prize specimens and keep a careful eye on the pond for the next few days.

Pests

The largest pest is usually the heron, a fishing bird with a decidedly fine taste for garden pond fishes; it arrives just after dawn and clears a pond of prize fishes before the owner is awake. Some keepers cover their pond with a fine net, placed well above the surface to prevent the bird's beak from going through the mesh and spearing the fishes. Whether it is the difficulty of reaching a fish and swallowing it through the net, or the fear that the bird is going to be caught in the mesh, is not really known, but most pond owners find this method effective. Another and less unsightly remedy is to restrict the bird's flight path; poles placed close together will prevent the wings from spreading, and encourage the bird to look for an easier and safer meal. Black thread stretched over the pond and its surround can achieve a similar effect without spoiling the look of the pond.

Cats too are attracted to the movement and flavour of garden fishes. They can be prevented by netting, or by a pet dog. A quick shower of cold water from a garden hose is a harmless deterrent.

Insect pests
Most of the insect life found in ponds is in some way harmful to plants or fishes, but this is part of nature and provided the damage is minimal the whole cycle of life will continue. But where there is some imbalance, and one insect becomes too numerous, then remedial action is necessary.

Several types of beetles and their larvae can be considered pests in the garden pond. One to look out for is the Great Diving Beetle, *Dytiscis marginalis*. It is hard to miss this rapacious predator; the adult may grow to a length of 4cm (1.6in), its dark brown oval body sometimes margined in yellow. Using its powerful mandibles, this beetle will rapidly and with the utmost of selfless ferocity attack fishes larger than itself. The larva, up to 5cm (2in) in length, is even more voracious.

Among the harmful water bugs that are able to fly from pond to pond are the so-called Water Boatmen or Backswimmers, *Notonecta* sp., easily recognizable by their upside-down swimming action just beneath the water's surface. *Notonecta glauca*, up to 1.5cm (0.6in) long, is the most commonly seen species. The Water Scorpion, *Nepa cinerea*, also attacks fishes and tadpoles. Up to 3cm (1.2in) long, this water bug has a terminal tube that it uses for breathing and is easily mistaken for a scorpion-like sting. All these water bugs and beetles are difficult to eliminate.

In many cases, it is the larval stages that pose the strongest threat to pond fishes. This is certainly true of Dragonflies, for their larvae (nymphs) lie low in submerged burrows and pounce on pond creatures that venture too close. They will attack fishes up to their own length – about 5cm (2in) – and are difficult to eradicate.

Leeches
Among those parasites that can be accidentally introduced with fishes or plants are the leeches. These worm-like animals are common in fresh water and grip their victims by means of suckers at each end of the body. They suck blood and may leave wounds that weaken the fishes and make them susceptible to other infections. Several treatments for these parasites are now commonly available. Many of them, however, are specific to single forms of pond life.

Fish lice, anchor worm and flukes
Fish lice (*Argulus* sp.) and anchor worms (*Lernaea cyprinacea*) are both parasitic crustaceans that grip onto or burrow into the fish's skin. The disc-shaped fish louse reaches up to 8mm (0.3in) in diameter and has two large gripping suckers. The anchor worm, up to 2cm (0.8in) long, penetrates the body tissue by means of jagged anchor-like appendages and can cause considerable wounds.

Both these parasites may cause affected fish to swim rapidly around the pond. Similar 'distress symptoms' are also seen in fishes carrying gill flukes (*Dactylogyrus* sp.). These are flatworm parasites up to 0.8mm (0.03in) long that attach themselves to the gill membranes. Skin flukes (*Gyrodactylus*) may also cause problems. Use an anti-parasite remedy for both these flukes.

Black spot

This is caused by the sucking worm *Neodiplostomum cuticola*. In this case it is the larval stage that produces the symptoms – brown or black spots on the body or fins. Each spot is an encysted larva. This parasite may be introduced by snails or visiting birds, and is best treated with an anti-parasite remedy.

Below: *The main pests to look for.* Top left: *Aphids on aquatic plants can carry diseases.* Right: *Water beetles can damage plants and attack fish.*

Plant pests

Aquatic plants, particularly water lilies, can become infested with aphids and other small insects. If your pond is well stocked with fishes, just push the leaves under the water and rest a piece of wood over them to keep the leaves immersed. The fishes will eat the pests, and the leaves can then be released.

Bottom row, left to right: *The Anchor Worm, Dragonfly larvae and Fish Louse will all attack or attach themselves to fish, causing damage.*

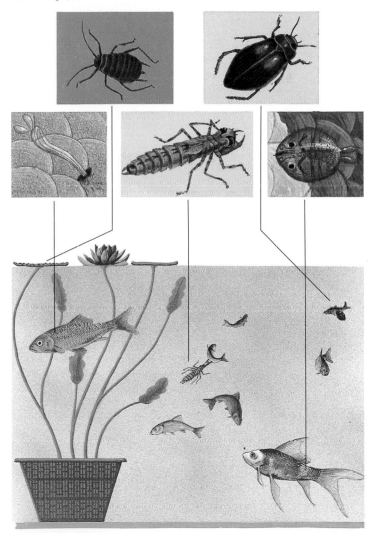

Diseases

Most diseases only attack fish in a weakened condition, and can be averted by simple husbandry. Most diseases occur in spring when the fish are coming out of their inactive period with reduced resistance, or in the autumn because they have not been properly treated during the summer.

It is important to build up energy reserves from midsummer onwards. Besides using good quality fish foods, a lump of cooked porridge, as much as can be consumed in 15 minutes, is beneficial. If the pond is cleaned at the end of the season and is deep enough for the fish to avoid the ice, disease-resistance should be high.

Fungus

This is one of the most common problems. It is caused by *Saprolegnia*, a fungus which produces tufts of long (usually white) fibres attached to the fish. Physically damaged or weakened fishes are particularly prone to infection. Treatment using a proprietary remedy is effective and can be carried out in the pool.

Finrot

Sometimes a fish appears to have been attacked by other fishes, with its tail and fins ragged. This may be the result of a bacterial infection that slowly disintegrates the fins, leaving only tattered fin rays. The disease starts at the extremities and gradually spreads towards the body. It is usually prevalent in long-finned

Below: *This Goldfish has damage to the head and back, probably due to poor handling, and will become more susceptible to disease*

coldwater fishes when the water temperature has been consistently below 10°C (50°F). Effectively cures are available, but prevention lies in the hands of the fishkeeper.

Ulcers

This is one of the most intractable conditions and is believed to be brought on mainly by stress. Ulcerated patches appear on the fish's body, as if the flesh had been eaten away. It is best overcome by maintaining clean conditions. Try proprietary remedies and painting the ulcers with Friar's Balsam.

White spot

This common parasitic affliction shows as small white spots all over the fins and body. It should not be confused with the white tubercles that appear on the gills and pectoral fins of male Goldfishes in the breeding season. Proprietary anti-parasite remedies are effective.

Dropsy

Occasionally a fish has its scales projecting, with an overall bloated look and protruding eyes. This condition, dropsy, is a rare disease that can now be treated using proprietary anti-ulcer products.

Plant diseases

Plant diseases are caused by various infections and as most grow in water it is difficult to treat them without polluting the pond. It is better to remove the plant and treat it out of the pond. If this is not possible, destroy the diseased plant and replace it with a new one. Most diseases are caused through damage to the plant under

the water or through a soil-borne infection; make sure that soils are sterilized before planting.

Bog plants are susceptible to rot when the water level rises too high in the soil; although they need a lot of moisture, once the air is removed there is a danger of root rot.

Fungal attacks should be treated with a fungicide suitable for pond surrounds, and the maker's instructions should be followed. It is often better to paint the plant with the treatment than to use a spray, to lower any risk of the fungicide drifting into the pond. Any diseased leaves should be removed and burnt to lessen the risk of disease spreading to neighbouring growth, and dead leaves should be removed in autumn.

Below: *Some of the pond diseases. Top row, left to right: Fin and tail rot, a progressive disease; root rot attacks the root system; and fungus on fish that appears as tufts or fur. Lower left: Dropsy, an incurable disease. Right: Leaf spot, which needs to be treated to stop it spreading to other leaves.*

A seasonal diary

Spring

Spring shows itself when the bulbs begin to appear and the fishes in the pond begin to stir, rising to the surface and moving in search of food. You can start to feed them but give only a very little at a time; use the floating pellets so that you can be sure that no more are given than the fishes can eat in five minutes or so. The first flowers of the aquatics should be blooming, usually *Caltha palustris* (the Marsh Marigold) in both single and double forms. The water lilies should be making growth, sending up shoots through the water. Frogs and other amphibians will begin to mate and spread their spawn in the shallow parts of the pond.

As the fishes have used up most of their reserves of nutrition they have little resistance to disease, particularly fungus infections. They need to be nurtured until their energy increases, and then their food should be supplemented with minced earthworms and scraps of meat and vegetables. Give the fishes as much as they will eat to bring them up to good condition ready for breeding.

Sometimes the decaying vegetation and the plant growth of the oxygenators and other aquatics that died back during the winter make the water coloured, sometimes black and at other times cloudy. This is more likely to happen in small ponds where there has been a prolific aquatic plant growth. The decaying matter should be removed where possible, and a partial water change is often necessary. There are two basic methods of changing the water. The easiest is to allow the fresh water to trickle in from a hosepipe and the excess water to overflow the edge of the pond very gently; this is fine where the surrounding soil is quick-draining and the water will not cause any hazard. The alternative is to drain half the water out of the pond into a soakaway or drain by using a pump and hose. Once the pond is down to half full the hose can be attached to the tap and adjusted to give a gentle trickle. If your tap water is highly chlorinated, get a dechlorinator from your aquarist suppliers, to make the water more palatable for the fishes.

The trickle action will give the water time to adjust to the surrounding temperature.

While the pool is at a low ebb, it is wise to take out and check the plant life. Baskets can be raised, and where the plants are too rampant divide and replant them. Replace weak plants, and remove those that are too vigorous and tall, putting smaller-growing varieties in their place.

Equipment removed in the autumn can be checked and put back into the pond. Examine everything for wear, and the cables for chafing or cracking, replacing where necessary. Check the connections to make sure

that they are secure. Grease the pins on plugs to ensure a good contact, and service pumps and lights if they require it. Check light bulbs and replace any that do not work. Clean out the filter, and see that the impeller on the pump is working freely; then start the pump working for a short while to make sure that everything is in order for the summer. After the danger of frost has passed, the pool heater can be removed and stored for the summer. Clean netting of old leaves, and restretch it to keep off herons and cats; make sure that the edges are well secured as these predators have been known to lift a loose end and enjoy a free meal of fish in comparative freedom.

When feeding plants around the perimeter of the pond, take care to prevent any spillage of fertilizer into the water, as it will encourage algae. It is better to use a natural organic food such as well-rotted manure or a liquid feed based on seaweed rather than a chemically based one that may leave excess nitrates in the soil that can seep into the pond water.

Below: *Spring flowers and emerging growth show the beginnings of a fresh season: the time to check the plants and start feeding the fish.*

Summer

Summer is the time to enjoy the pond, to watch the action and movement, to savour the fragrance of the flowers and listen to the sounds of water and insect life. The various aquatics are flowering; the water lilies start in warm weather with their cup-shaped flowers on and above the water surface, the marginals and bog plants a little less spectacularly.

Some plants need thinning during the summer months to prevent them from becoming too large for their allotted space. When this entails lifting the basket to cut back side shoots or to divide it, the water becomes muddy, and this can take a day or two to settle. But switch on the pump for the fountain or waterfall, and the filter will strain out the silt, so that the water will become less cloudy within an hour or two. New plants can be settled in, and old ones tidied up and fed with aquatic fertilizer pellets to boost their growth, especially the water lilies. Where insects have attacked leaves just above the water surface, push down the affected parts under the water and rest a plank or weight on them to keep them immersed while the fishes eat the insects as a bonus live feed.

This is the time of year when a rapid and unexpected growth of filamentous algae – usually called blanket weed – can occur, even in ponds that have been free from it for

Above: *The splash of moving water with the colour and scent of flowers on a hot summer's day is only part of the reward for having a pool.*

Left: *Lush green growth of waterside plants will attract colourful insects on hot days, and cool the oppressive heat of the midsummer sun.*

decades. Some say that this is due to amphibians arriving at the pond with tiny strands of the weed caught round their legs or bodies from another pond; when they swim the strand becomes loose and spreads speedily in its new environment. Insert a stout pole into the mass of green leaf and turn it; like a fork in a plateful of spaghetti, it will gather up all the weed, which can then be lifted out and removed.

The fishes become more active and need a supplement to their food if the insect life is not too prolific; but do not allow the food to stay in the pond to spoil and pollute the water. If the fishes have spawned and the tiny fry are seen swimming about, separate the young from their parents to prevent their being eaten. Take out the fry with a very fine net and keep them in a separate pond until they are large enough to rejoin their parents. New fishes should be kept in quarantine before being released into the pond; the plastic bag in which they have travelled should be immersed in a container or a separate pond until it is certain that the fishes are healthy and vigorous, when they can be moved into the main pond. One diseased fish can cause havoc in an otherwise healthy pond.

If evaporation occurs during hot weather the level should be topped up and the fountain or waterfall should be working most of the time.

Autumn

Plants are beginning to look tired, and as soon as the first frost occurs many will be cut back. This is the time to remove dead withering leaves and growth, and seed heads should be removed unless you want the plants to seed. The plants in the pond, particularly those with leaves under the surface, should be cut well back

Below: At the end of the winter the pool hints at the promise of spring with fresh growth just emerging.

Above: *In winter the spectacle of frost and ice is beautiful, but some water should be kept open for fish.*

and the growth removed. The exceptions to this are the evergreen plants, which should have their dying leaves removed. This will lessen any decay of plant life in the pond and avoid upsetting its balance. Spent leaves and blooms of water lilies should also be removed. Any tender plants that will not survive the frost must be lifted and removed to a frost-

to catch the fish. As cooler weather comes, the fishes will be less active. The more delicate specimens should be carefully lifted out and put into a frost-free pond or aquarium indoors for the winter. As most of the natural cover for the fishes has now been removed or allowed to die back, some form of shelter is essential to give them protection during the winter months when they are slow and in a near hibernation state – an ideal quarry for a predator. Lay a series of inert drain pipes on the pool bottom, in which the fishes will be able to hide and remain secure from the attentions of herons and cats. Protect pond-side plants that are not quite hardy by covering them with a layer of bracken or straw.

free place. The pond should be cleared of rotting vegetation.

Fishes should be fattened up; give them plenty of food so that they can have a good store of nutrients to help them through the winter months. They should still be active as long as the weather remains warm, but make sure that no food is left in the water to decompose.

Check that the edges of the pond net are secure, and that it will catch any leaves that fall towards the pond and also deter predators from trying

Winter

In cold weather the fishes need less oxygen and food, and they rest in a state of torpor gradually using up the food stored as layers of fat. When the pond freezes over it keeps oxygen from reaching the water and prevents the toxic gases from leaving it. For the most part the cold is only sufficient for the pond to be frozen over for a few hours, and this is not a hazard to the pond inhabitants. Only when it is covered with ice for a number of days does trouble start to build up.

A pond heater is an ideal answer; drop it into the water, where its float will bring it to the surface. The little power that it uses – the equivalent of an electric-light bulb – will be sufficient to keep an area of water free from ice. Switch it on only when frost is forecast, and keep it on in times of prolonged freezing. An alternative is to fill a can with boiling water and rest it on the ice, which will soon melt. Remove some of the water from under the ice, to leave a gap for air to get in and for the gases to get out.

Remove and clean pumps, then store them for the winter should the makers advise it. If a pump is left in the pond it is important to run it for a few minutes every week or so, to keep the machine parts free and working well. Pond lights should also be removed and cleaned; remove algae from the glass, check the wiring, and store the lights for the whole winter period.

Index to Plants, Fishes and Livestock

Numbers in *italics* refer to illustrations.
Text entries are shown in normal type.

Picture Credits

Artists
Copyright of the artwork illustrations on the pages following the artists' names is the property of Salamander Books Ltd.

Dee McLain (Linden Artists): 36, 38-9, 40-1, 42-3, 45, 46
Clifford and Wendy Meadway: 16, 17, 18-9, 20, 22, 23, 26-7, 64, 65, 66, 68, 70, 100-1, 102-3, 105, 107
Colin Newman (Linden Artists): 52-3, 54-5, 56-7, 58-9, 60-1, 62-3, 72-3, 74-5, 77
David Papworth: 29, 30-1, 32, 34-5, 48-9, 50-1

Photographs
The publishers wish to thank the following photographers and agencies who have supplied photographs for this book. The photographs have been credited by page number and position on the page: (B) Bottom, (T) Top, (BL) Bottom left etc.

Heather Angel/Biofotos: 94, 96
British Koi-Keeper's Society: 90, 91 (TL, TR)
Michael Chinery: 97, 98, 99
Bruce Coleman Ltd: 17(T, Eric Crichton), 76-7(Hans Reinhard), 83(Jane Burton), 86-7(Hans Reinhard)
Eric Crichton: 38-9, 112-13 © Salamander Books Ltd: Endpapers, 12, 88
Bob Gibbons Photography: 64, 65, 66(B), 67, 69(BL)
Jerry Harpur: Title page (Stonestacks Turton), copyright page, 10-11 (Designer: Peter Rogers), 13, 14-15, 21 (Designer: Mark Rumary), 23 (Designer: Paul Temple), 24-5 (Designer: Valery Stevenson), 30-1 (Designer: James van Sweden), 33 (Designer: Peter Rogers), 34-5 (Designer: Valery Stevenson) 37 (Designer: John Vellam), 40-1, 42-3 (Designer: Vic Shanley), 44-5, 46-7(T), 47(B) (Designer: John Vellam), 49(T) (Designer: Alex Rota), 51(BL), 108-9(York Gate), 110-11
Ideas into Print: 80(T), 89(T), 91(B)
Dick Mills: 106
Arend van den Nieuwenhuizen: 82, 89(B)
Barry Pengilley: 79, 80-1(B), 81(T), 84, 84-5, 87(Inset)
Laurence Perkins: 68, 78, 92-3, 95(C)
Mike Sandford: 95(T)
Michael Warren: Half title page, 28, 66(C), 69(BR), 70, 71

Editorial assistance
Copy-editing Maureen Cartwright

Acknowledgements
The publishers would like to thank the following for their assistance in preparing ths book: The British Koi-Keeper's Society; David Everett, Anglo Aquarium Plant Company Ltd, Interpet Ltd; Stapeley Water Gardens; David Quelch, Waterworld.

A formal patio pond